COLLINS FIELD GUIDE

# BIRD SONGS & CALLS

of Britain & Northern Europe

COLLINS FIELD GUIDE

# BIRD SONGS & CALLS

of Britain & Northern Europe

Geoff Sample

HarperCollins*Publishers*

## ACKNOWLEDGEMENTS

Thanks to Roger Boughton, Simon Elliott, Phil Hollom, Charles and Heather Myers, Richard Savage and Chris Watson for supplying additional recordings.

HarperCollins*Publishers*
77-85 Fulham Palace Road
London
W6 8JB

First published 1996

00

10  9  8  7

The author hereby asserts his moral right to be identified as the author of this work and the publisher undertakes to observe such assertion and to impose the same condition on its licencees

ISBN 0 00 220037 6

Manufactured in the UK for Imago

# CONTENTS

# INTRODUCTION

Over the last decade I have become a devoted student of bird song; I was fortunate in that, since I was working as an engineer and producer in the music business, I already had access to some professional recording equipment and digital technology was just sweeping through the audio world. Once I had made a few decent recordings of some things I was interested in, I was smitten; being able to replay events one has witnessed, and listen more closely to the details of sounds that are otherwise very ephemeral, was wonderful. Now, ornithology had been in my blood from a very young age and, not being one to do things by halves, I decided to call a halt to recording music, get the best equipment for the purpose and pursue bird song full time as best I could. Pretty rash in the middle of the recent recession.

To make matters worse, I was drawn to recording birds in a particular way - I wanted the full picture, as I heard it. This meant a more ambient approach than traditional wildlife recording, which seeks to capture an individual's calls with minimal extraneous sounds. Such recordings are obviously of scientific interest and convenient for TV dubbing; but for me there is much of interest in the context of the sound, in terms of both the bird community and the acoustics of the place.

North-west Europe is a densely populated area, full of the hum and drone of distant machines and, as I found, wildlife recordists get to know noise intimately - as they say, know your enemy. You begin to keep odd hours and hang around lonely places, staring into space (listening, that is) for long periods, accompanied by bundles of electronic gadgetry - or so it appears to fellow humans. Yet the privilege is immense: the intimate experiences with wildlife and so many wonderful dawns and sunsets. When recording, I become a man of the twilight.

I am very grateful to Myles Archibald at HarperCollins for taking up the challenge and giving me the opportunity to put a work like this together. Thanks are due for generous assistance and advice over the years to various wardens and officers of the RSPB, Scottish Natural Heritage and English Nature. I should also acknowledge the dedicated band of recordists, some of whom have contributed recordings to the work, and others who have shared their knowledge in discussion. Nevertheless I have had a free rein and any mistakes or errors are mine - it's a big subject, in which the traditional explanations are not always complete, and I'm still learning.

There was a limit to the number of species we could include; and naturally this has led to reluctant omissions. If something you are particularly fond of, or wanted to hear, has not been included, remember that something else would have had to have been omitted. For the technically-minded, the recordings as presented were not all consecutive; recordings from similar locations or different times at the same location have been edited together.

Learning bird sounds is not easy: inevitably it takes time and, more than anything else, experience in the field. There are many species in our region alone, often with wide vocabularies and variable songs. But getting to know a few species common in a local habitat is not difficult.

And the rewards for a little perseverance are immense. For the birder, there's species recognition: after a long day in the reed-beds, the characteristic 'pings' of the Bearded Tit may be the key to a good sighting of this unobtrusive bird. So often sound proves the vital clue to the presence of secretive birds like the Water Rail or the Quail. But it offers more: it offers a more intimate knowledge of birds daily lives, different species' behaviour patterns - their character, if you like. And to anyone with musical ears who enjoys being out of doors, a little learning could enrich the experience greatly. Surely few people are unimpressed on first hearing a Nightingale singing in the dead of night. Well, there's a wealth of other talent out there - and it's free.

Any discussion of bird song inevitably includes much generalisation, if it is not to become long-winded; but there is so much variation between species, populations and individuals that each such generalisation has its exceptions - there are no absolute rules. Chiff-chaffs occasionally produce 'aberrant', Willow Warbler-like songs and frequently produce songs which sound more like a 3-note motif than the eponymous 'chiff-chaff'. Nightjars are largely nocturnal, but churring is occasionally heard in the day. Marsh Warblers sing for a short period, hardly more than the month of June; nonetheless a few years ago a bird was found singing in September in Britain. If this makes the subject sound overwhelmingly complex, remember there is much repetition and sound must have a recognisable pattern to work in communication. In short, I apologise for all the oftens, generallys and usuallys in the text, but they are unavoidable if it is to remain accurate. Science seeks to recognise patterns and establish rules, but the living world has variation built in - leading to biodiversity.

Geoff Sample Northumberland January, 1996

# WHAT'S IT ALL ABOUT ?

In general conversation the term 'bird song' is often used to refer to bird sounds as a whole, certainly the more pleasant ones. Looking at the subject further, we quickly come to recognise the traditional distinction between songs and calls: the repeated, sharp 'tic' call of an alert and nervous Robin is obviously a quite different kind of vocalisation from its song, with elaborate melodic patterns and no obvious immediate function in the bird's behaviour; the bird seems to sing for the sake of singing. Calls are often single notes, sometimes simple motifs and usually given in more or less specific situations. On the other hand there are some species, notably in the tit family, where it is difficult to distinguish between calls and songs on the form of the vocalisation alone: the 'pi-tchou' call of the Marsh Tit and its variations are more elaborate sounds than the repeated single note of the male's usual song. The distinctive boom of the Bittern, a single low note repeated several times, has the simplicity of a call; and the commonest Pheasant call heard is probably the male's crowing for territory and status - not usually thought of as a song. And what of the 'reeling' of the Grasshopper Warbler or the 'churring' of the Nightjar ? Yet the males of these species are behaving in much the same way as a male Chaffinch in song.

So the use of the term 'song' has always had an element of aesthetic evaluation: the more elaborate (and often tuneful) breeding vocalisations of the 'true' song-birds being heard as songs. There is however a more scientific basis to the distinction if we investigate the functions of different types of vocal behaviour, but we must expand our musical horizons. In the breeding season, individual birds, usually the males, perform with sound often for long periods to claim a breeding space and attract and stimulate a mate. Such vocalisation is often loud and elaborate. Outside the sexual and territorial context, birds tend to call with simpler sounds, often single notes, and often with different calls for particular circumstances, such as contact in flight and warning of a predator. Many of the passerines have sexual calls used by breeding pairs, quite distinct from the male's song. It is true of the passerines generally that their breeding vocalisations have developed a formal elaboration beyond most of the non-passerines and they have a more complex musculature to the syrinx (the bird's vocal organ) - hence the idea of 'true song-birds'. In terms of behaviour, the Bittern booming in Spring is singing in his own way; sometimes such songs have been called song-substitutes (cf also the Capercaillie) or breeding calls. For myself, I tend to use the term 'song' loosely to cover breeding and territorial vocal displays (and, of course, practising to sing): it is defined more by the performance than the sound. Song is essentially sexual. Why songs that sound pleasant to us have developed in so many species is a different, but very interesting question.

## TERMINOLOGY

Bird calls are frequently referred to in literature with phonetic representations and often these get used as a kind of name for the type of call. While this is very useful, it can also be misleading if interpreted too strictly. With the fine degree of 'enunciation' available to birds and the variations found between individuals, the same or similar calls might sound like both 'pip' or 'chk' (cf Greater Spotted Woodpecker 1,59) on different instances or to different listeners; they are not always descriptively accurate and different observers use different terms for the same type of call. Remember to treat them as approximations; hearing is a subjective experience, which we have not developed an accurate language for describing.

In using such phonetics, syllables without vowels tend to be staccato calls, with a percussive, often harmonically-complex waveform. Vowels tend to be an indication of a definite pitch, with two vowels indicating a change in pitch: 'ui' suggesting a rising pitch change, 'eeoo' a descending one. A hyphen between the vowels would suggest there are almost two separate syllables or notes. A 'y' is often an indication of a sudden slide in pitch; thus 'whee-yoo' should refer to a disyllabic call holding a high pitch briefly, then with a quick slide a lower one, sustained briefly.

Mnemonics (memorising aids) have been used to refer to various birds' songs; 'wet my lips' for the Quail's song and 'a little bit of bread with no chee-eese' for the yellowhammer's. These are usually suggestive of the rhythm of the song more than the sound of the notes.

'Trill' is a term frequently used in describing bird sounds: for good examples of trills listen to the Greenfinches (1,21) or the Wood Warbler (1,82). 'Churring' is another term I use frequently for what sounds like a fast, regular run of notes (like a trill, but more run-together): for examples listen to the Nightjar's song (1,48), the Wren's second alarm call (1,76) or the Whitethroat's alarm call (1,33)

## CALLS

We have established that there is not always a clear distinction between songs and calls per se, but that calls tend to be single notes or simple motifs, and often short; in terms of behaviour and communication, information in a call tends to be related to the immediate circumstances of the caller. We tend to speak of a species' vocabulary of calls, as if they were different words, and for some species this can extend to 15 or more items, though distinctions between some calls can be rather fine. We can distinguish between different types of call in many of the passerines and some of the non-passerines fairly easily; but other passerines, such as the corvids or to some extent the pipits, and many non-passerines tend to use the same voice in different situations with varying simple, repetitive motifs, articulation and intensity. It may be more difficult to perceive different types of call in such vocalisation, but that does not mean a limited range of expression.

Begging calls from nestlings and placatory calls from parents are general in most species. Aggressive calls are general across species, developed by siblings in the nest, but are more common in adults of species prone to flocking or feeding together. Aggressive calls may be directed at other species and other kinds of animal, including man (cf Arctic Tern 2,74). Birds call to keep in contact with each other; many of the passerines have specific calls whose function seems little more than keeping in touch - 'contact calls'. Contact calls are common in maintaining a flock and frequent in species that forage in pairs or loose parties. Territorial birds of some species (eg Chaffinch) have calls which they repeat for periods within their territory, usually referred to as 'territorial calls', though the distiction between a territorial call and song can get somewhat blurred.

Many species have one or more particular calls they give when anxious to varying degrees; an anxious bird, in a state of alarm, might give a fairly loud, scolding call and these are often referred to as 'alarm calls' (cf Wren 1,76); though there may not be the intention to send a warning to other birds, that is one of the consequences. Such warning calls do occur in flock alerts and frequently as predator-warnings in the passerines. One common type of such calls is a high, thin, descending whistle, given in similar forms by various passerine species of different families, such as Blackbirds, Blue Tits and Chaffinches; such sounds, high-pitched and pure of tone, are difficult to locate and these warning calls tend to be given, for instance, when a hawk flies near - obviously the individual does not want to draw attention to itself. Many other kinds of alarm calls, including mobbing calls, tend to be short and harmonically rich, making them easier to locate and drawing attention to both bird and intruder. Many species have calls associated with flight, often given both in flight and signalling a bird's intention to fly. Flight calls can be similar within families, but are useful to learn, since it is not always easy to pick up visual characteristics of flying birds.

Such categories are helpful in recognising and understanding something of the significance of bird calls, but they should not be taken too strictly. Often a call type can be given with repeated, slight variations and suddenly you're hearing a different call type (cf Meadow Pipit 2,07); and it has been shown that the same call, given in a different context, may have a changed significance. It may be linguistically simple, but the way the system works is often subtle and complex. It is best to begin with a species' most common and distinct calls and accept the usual interpretation; and undoubtedly the most common calls we hear are alarm calls of one form or another, as birds react to our approach.

## SONG

*Seasonality*

Few birds sing throughout the year and some have very restricted song periods; singing has been found to be linked with levels of the hormone testosterone in birds. This hormone controls sexual activity ('if music be the food of love...'). In some species birds have quite high levels in the Autumn, but for most species the increasing daylight in the Spring triggers a rise in their testosterone levels and they begin to sing regularly with their full song. In terms of light, Spring builds from the Winter solstice; on bright or mild days, birds of an increasing number of species can be heard singing and displaying through the latter part of Winter.

In some species, such as the Pied Flycatcher, song pretty well ceases once the male has found a mate; for many species singing becomes less frequent, less intense and less formal. In general there is a quiet period in mid Summer with breeding over and many birds moulting. But there is also a smaller peak in the testosterone levels of many species in the early Autumn and this too correlates with the observed seasonality of song; in a number of species there is a resumption of song for a while in the back-end and some of the migrants, like the Willow Warbler, can be heard singing occasionally as they make their way south. There is some suggestion that much of the song heard in the Autumn is from young birds, but I suspect this will vary between species. So far so good; but Robins are an interesting case. In the Autumn and Winter male and female Robins hold separate territories and both sexes sing. Like most species levels of testosterone in the males reach a peak in the Spring, but not apparently in the Winter; on the other hand levels of this hormone in the females rise in the Autumn. As I said earlier, there are no absolute rules.

*Sexuality*

In general it is the males that sing, though females of some species occasionally do so, and some species indulge in the mutual stimulation of duets. Not all songs are produced vocally: most Woodpeckers and the Common Snipe 'sing' with mechanically-produced sounds - both comfusingly known as drumming. Behavioural research points to a dual function in singing: to defend a territory and attract a mate. In most species breeding territories are established and pairs formed by one of the birds, usually the male, performing with song to advertise his claim; since this is of little interest to individuals of other species, it is to each species' benefit to have its own distinctive voice and sound patterns.

The singer broadcasts, through his performance in full song, his species identity and indications of his condition and sexual status. Neighbours come to recognise his individual identity in the particular songs he uses and his voice. I find the idea of status is useful: singing confers status on the singer, which may enable him to establish and defend a breeding territory and attract and keep a mate. In this way birds have evolved a less expensive way of disputing boundaries and mating rights than physical violence with its risk of injury and high energy requirements. Sometimes such disputes still arise, particularly in lekking birds. But there is also evidence of a stimulatory function; the increased vocal activity and the kinds of vocalisation help the development of breeding physiology and behaviour. The courtship factor is strong.

*Learning*

When Spring comes, a first year bird does not suddenly find within itself a fine rendition of the species' song: a certain amount of learning and practise is necessary. Some calls, the specific kind of voice and a certain 'blueprint' of the species' song seem to be inherited characteristics; but without hearing other adult's songs a young bird does not seem to be able to develop the full characteristic song of the species. In calling this 'full song' we are distinguishing it from the experimental practising sessions of a young bird (cf Chaffinch 1,68) and the softer, less formally-structured singing that occasionally occurs in courtship (cf Bullfinch 1,65 or Spotted Flycatcher 1,83); this has been called 'subsong' and is usually much quieter and more varied (often a warble) than full song. Birds are sometimes heard in subsong in the Autumn. Full song has also been called 'primary song', 'advertising song' and 'broadcasting song'; subsong does not have the broadcasting significance of full song. Despite the pejorative connotations in the term, I find subsong one of the most fascinating areas of bird song, by nature experimental and, when it occurs in courtship, inventive and excited.

With practice, the young bird usually begins to deliver the characteristic species song sometime in it's first breeding Spring, in versions learnt from the other adults around it and often some versions developed itself. Adults of most species have more than one version of their song in their repertoire and birds tend to change song-types in an extended bout of singing. The size of a bird's repertoire varies from individual to individual and species to species. Because the young bird learns from the other birds around him, the possibility of vocal characteristics and song-types specific to that population or group arises; with more sedentary and site-faithful species this may have a distinct geographical basis and lead to what have been called 'local dialects'. Where a population becomes geographically isolated from the rest of its species, conditions allow distinctive vocalisations to develop and other aspects of the process of speciation to begin (consider the Scottish Crossbill). Certainly there is cultural tradition in bird song, and the songs of Wrens in Galloway contain different elements and phrasing from the Wrens on the Northumberland coast. But it is just as likely that any of these elements might crop up again in a Wren population in Greece.

As regards maintaining a territory and attracting a mate, for those species in which territorial behaviour is strong and the males maintain mutually exclusive territories, singing tends to be loud, frequent, formal and distinctive over the broadcasting distance (cf Chaffinch 1,25 or Song Thrush 1,93). But for species with closer social breeding systems, in distinct or loose colonies, there is less need for the song to be loud and formal (cf House Sparrow 1,2 or Greenfinch 1,21). Territorial species' songs tend to be more stereotyped and those of less territorial species more meandering and elaborate; but it's been found that even in the latter case, with birds like the Sedge Warbler, the Garden Warbler or the Nightingale, all individuals have a basic repertoire of elements from which their songs are built.

*Mimicry*

Imitating others is intrinsic to the process of a young bird (and most other young animals, for that matter) learning the vocal and other display rituals of its species; conforming to an idiom plays a role in bonding individuals into a cohesive social unit. But with birds mimicry goes further. Many species are prone to working imitations of other species calls and songs into their own songs. Starlings are well-known for their skills in this respect (cf 1,3) and some of the warblers, like Sedge Warblers (cf 2,22 and 2,27), Marsh Warbler and Blackcap; Blackbirds, Song Thrushes and some of the chats, especially Winchats (cf 2,3) and Redstarts, at times produce superb imitations of other species. It is thought that most imitations are learnt from others of a bird's own species, rather than the species being copied, though obviously one has to copy the original in the first place. It is interesting to note that often the calls are imitated as they are heard rather than as delivered - that's to say the imitation of a Pheasant call sounds like a Pheasant call in the distance, often with acoustic colouration, rather than the sound of a Pheasant calling where the imitator is perched. The Shrike species and Jays are also quite prone to mimicry; with these species the imitations tend to have a specific tonal colouration.

## LANGUAGE & COMMUNICATION

Acoustic communication has certain advantages over sight and smell and developed in several early kinds of animal, but not to any great degree. Sound signals are good over a reasonably long range, they can negotiate obstacles, they are reasonably locatable, they are constantly variable and exist for as long as the source wants. Fish sense physical vibrations (the basis of sound) but do not have an ear or any specific organ for making sounds; many species of insect 'sing' to attract a mate, notably the orthopterans (grasshoppers and crickets), but they produce their sounds mechanically with scraping movements and hear with tympanic membranes in their legs - simple ears. Many species of frogs and toads also sing to attract a mate; their croakings show a wide variety, but are hardly as elaborate and the ability in the individual to articulate a range of sounds has not developed. Voices, ears and more elaborate acoustic communication have only developed in mammals and birds (and dinosaurs ..?). And it has been said that vocal communication has reached its highest development in birds - apart from Man, that is.

Environmental factors have had some influence on the evolution of the kinds of sound we hear from birds. The varying physical make-up of different habitats affects the clarity of sound transmission in that space and differents species' voices have evolved in the context of their own habitats. It has been found that on average the frequency content of forest birds' voices is significantly lower and they tend to purer tones than species of open habitats; the exact reasons for this are unclear, but certainly lower pitches and pure tones exploit the resonance of the forest. The rapid frequency modulation commoner in open habitat species' voices tends to become unclear in woodland, distorted by the reflected sound that gives a forest its resonance. Some habitats feature higher levels of background noise: the Dipper's voice has evolved to the backdrop of running water.

*Socialising*

They say birds of a feather flock together; and this same propensity for socially co-ordinated behaviour is largely paralleled in the vocal activity of individual species and associations of species. Communication helps coordinate the behaviour of individuals and avoid conflicts; sound signals can be quickly transmitted and quickly modified. Think of the constant twittering of a flock of Linnets or the way calls pass through a flock of geese like a mood. On the other hand one of the least social species, with a large home range, the Golden Eagle, is also one of the least vocal. Like many of the hawks and falcons, the Golden Eagle is a fairly solitary bird, with acute vision, and pairs need large areas to establish breeding territories; territorial birds advertise their presence with high display flights, visible for a great distance, much further than would be possible vocally. And hunting predators do not usually want to attract attention to themselves. But birds of many species are actually more vocal than we are aware. Watching from a distance you do not hear the softer 'chat' that often goes on between a pair or within a flock. Where a handbook refers to a species as rarely vocal, in many cases it would be more accurate to say rarely heard.

*Language*

The question of whether birds' vocal communication is a language has long attracted heated debate. In these post-modern times I would have thought there was no problem in accepting the term, in the same way that visual signalling, with posturing and ritualised movements, is said to have its own language. In birds, as in man, vocal communication is often synchronised with visual signals: there might be an element of threat display, begging or wings open to take flight, and usually some aspect of the plumage is emphasised.

But if the question is in the context of our verbal languages, based on complex syntactical codes which enable an infinite number of statements with discrete meanings to be made, there is no evidence of such a system in birds. Calls might be said to work with a simple code, providing several categories of statement; that's to say the same kinds of calls regularly crop up as contact calls, alarm calls, flight calls, warning calls and so on, especially within families and such calls often work between species. For such calls to be useful, the receptor must recognise the particular kind of call for what it is and thereby its significance.

In a sense, conversations take place between birds in a pair, a family or a flock, often with lengthy interchanges of calls; but there is no evidence of anything more than mutual appeasement, the calls often expressing balances of aggression and supplication. We might say that a call is repeated; often subsequent renditions are almost identical, but usually vary in expression. And therein lies the subtlety of their simple language - the slight variations in tone, intensity and pitch that express the state of mind, if you'll permit the term, of the bird at that moment.

## Research

Research on bird vocalisation has intensified over the last few decades. It has been helped by certain technological developments. Firstly accurate sound recording enabled the same sound to be listened to repeatedly and the ephemeral nature of sound was overcome; then the spectrographic analysis of sound enabled the details of particular sounds to be examined visually, overcoming the limited resolution of our hearing; finally general audio improvements coupled with a growing knowledge of animal behaviour have enabled sophisticated playback experiments to be conducted into birds' reactions to recordings in the field, providing an indication of the behavioural function of various sounds and ways of calling. There also used to be a certain amount of research using the controlled conditions of the laboratory - raising birds in small groups or in isolation and, regretably, occasionally involving deafening birds, to see the effects on their vocal development. But there is less of this kind of research now. Of course the results are not just of interest to ornithologists, but have enormous implications in the fields of animal behaviour and communication systems more generally.

A few years ago Peter McGregor made the news when, using sound spectrography to identify individual voice patterns, he established that there were probably no more than 16 male Bitterns booming in Britain; he found that the birds wander quite widely in large reed-bed territories, singing from different areas, and this had previously suggested the presence of several males.

# THE AUDIO

The 2 CDs contain 15 continuous pieces each covering a particular habitat.

## DISC 1

General Introduction (1)
Urban (2)
Gardens, Parks & Villages (13)
Farmland (30)
Heathland (45)
Lowland Woods (54)
Western Oakwood (72)
Northern Pinewood (85)

## DISC 2

Moorland (1)
Flow Country (12)
Wetlands (21)
Lakes & Ponds (37)
Rivers (54)
Summer Shore (65)
Winter Estuary (77)
Seacliff (91)

The numbers in brackets refer to track ID points on the CDs and take you to the start of the piece. Track ID numbers are also given for particular species singing or calling during the piece. Usually these 'drop you in' just before the relevant species begins, but sometimes the bird may have been singing for a while further off; occasionally two species are referenced with a single track number and there may be a short passage of something else before the bird you are listening for. Often a bird continues singing or calling after my identifying comments.

# DISC 1

## 01 URBAN Summer (8'52")

Despite all the rumble and din, cities are interesting places to listen to bird song. Starlings, Blackbirds and Song Thrushes have all been heard mimicking car alarms, burglar alarms and other electronic noises. Urban woodlands and parks are often in isolated pockets and local residential populations, especially Great Tits, often have some idiosyncratic songs. It seems that urban lighting and possibly the noise of nocturnal human activity stimulates Robins and sometimes Blackbirds to sing during the night. A few years ago on the 1st of February it seemed that all the territorial male Blackbirds in an area of South-East London were in song at 3 a.m., around 4 hours before dawn.

## 02 House Sparrow

Song of a male; male and female singing in courtship, prior to copulation. Various chirping calls can be heard from House Sparrows in the background elsewhere in this habitat piece.

## 03 Starling

Various whistling calls, leading into the full song of a single bird, including imitations of the calls of Grey Partridge, Lapwing, Common Gull and Curlew.

## 04 Blackbird

Song of a male. With House Sparrow calls in the background.

## 05 Black-headed Gull

Assertive calls from birds in a small party (c.6 birds) flying over the gardens on their daily circuit.

## 06 Carrion Crow

Calls from several birds.

## 07 Blackbird

Softer clucking calls of unease, building to sharper alarm calls, then the alarm rattle in flight.

## 08 Blue Tit

Songs with some variation and assertive call.

## 09 Feral Pigeon

Song of a male, or possibly several males, courting a female. With some Starling whistles in the background.

## 10 Pied Wagtail, Robin

'Chissik' flight calls of a Pied Wagtail; a Robin begins to sing (quite short song bursts, so possibly a bird busy with raising a family); variations on calls with a regular delivery from the Pied Wagtail - this seems to be the Pied Wagtail's form of territorial song.

## 11 Kestrel

Yikkering calls (usually attributed to the male, though I didn't identify the sex of the bird). With some 'caw's from a Carrion Crow.

## 12 Swift

Calls of several birds in aerial chases near a breeding site.

## 13 GARDENS, PARKS & VILLAGES Late Spring (12'26")

Often densely populated by a wide variety of passerine song bird species, this, probably our most familiar kind of habitat, is not the easiest for getting to grips with bird sounds. The air is often filled with the sounds of many different birds singing or calling at once, some true woodland species, and some species of more open habitats; and many of these adaptable and common species have quite wide vocabularies of calls.

## 13 Woodpigeon, Rook

Song of a male Wood Pigeon. Calls from several birds in a flock of Rooks passing over. With Bullfinch and Blue Tit in the background. Collared Doves and Wood Pigeons sing at intervals throughout this habitat piece.

## 14 Jackdaw

Calls from several birds in a party flying over. Jackdaws often loosely associate with Rooks in foraging flocks.

## 15 Great Tit

Song of a male: a common form of Great Tit song, though this one is thinner sounding and less resonant than usual.

## 16 Dunnock

Alarm or contact call: versions of this call, sometimes softer, at other times full as here, are used in various situations. 'Spink' calls and alarm churr of the Great Tit.

## 17 Collared Dove

Song of a male; then flight calls from several birds. With flight calls of a Goldfinch flitting about; and a Yellowhammer singing in the distance.

**18 Dunnock**
Song of a male; occasionally a second bird can be heard singing further off.

**19 Goldfinch**
Flight calls and song.

**20 Wren**
Song of a male; this bird or others can be heard singing at intervals throughout the piece. With Yellowhammer singing and Greenfinch and Goldfinch calls.

**21 Greenfinch**
Songs of 2 males - Greenfinch songs are built around variations of their calls.

**22 Swallow**
Calls of several birds in flight.

**23 Mistle Thrush, Swallow**
Alarm call of a Mistle Thrush; then a Swallow singing from a perch.

**24 Great Tit**
A different type of Great Tit song from 15, though possibly from the same bird.

**25 Chaffinch**
Song of a male; also some soft 'chiff' contact calls and a thin 'see' when taking flight. With Collared Dove and Wood Pigeon singing.

**26 Garden Warbler**
Song of a male, while foraging through the shrubbery. Wren and Chaffinch singing in the background.

**27 Magpie**
Calls from a pair. The Garden Warbler continues singing. Then a Blackcap singing closer, with Chaffinch, Wren and Starling in the background.

**28 Blackcap**
Song of a male: these are relatively elaborate and intense songs from the Blackcap (usually heard early in the breeding season or from birds that remain unmated) and quite similar in form to the Garden Warbler.

**29 House Martin**
Calls from birds of a flock in the air.

## 30 FARMLAND Late Spring (10'58")
Not as rich in bird life as it once was, farmland does still have some typical species, though you would be lucky to hear all these species in one area.

### 30 Skylark
Song of a male perched.

### 31 Barn Owl
Call of a male (it's hard to call such a sound a song). With Wren and Skylark singing.

### 32 Grey Partridge
Territorial and alarm or aggressive calls at c.250m. With Skylarks and Corn Bunting singing; then alarm calls of a Whitethroat close-by.

### 33 Whitethroat
Alarm calls from a pair.

### 34 Yellowhammer
Song of a male, with other males singing further away.

### 35 Corn Bunting
Song of a male. With the Yellowhammers continuing singing.

### 36 Whitethroat
Song of a male.

### 37 Quail
Territorial call at c.300m. With Yellowhammers singing.

### 38 Red-legged Partridge
Display calls. With Yellowhammer, Whitethroat and Grey Partridge.

### 39 Linnet
Various calls, including flight calls, from several birds.

### 40 Lesser Whitethroat
Song of a male. With Linnet calls; alarm call of Short-eared Owl.

### 41 Linnet
Song of a male. With other Linnets calling and Lesser Whitethroat singing further off.

### 42 Carrion Crow, Rook
Calls from several Carrion Crows; then Rook calls, continuing to the end of the piece; then 'whuit-whuit' calls from a Chaffinch briefly.

### 43 Tree Sparrow
Calls of a male. With Rooks and Coal Tit calls further off.

### 44 Yellow Wagtail
Song of a male.

### 45 HEATHLAND Early Summer (7'58")
Heathland is a wonderfully atmospheric habitat to visit in the twilight and you generally need to linger into the darkness or be out before dawn to hear Nightjars and Stone Curlews. As well as the species given here, many species of scrub, farmland and the woodland edge are found on heathland too.

### 45 Stone-curlew
Display calls from several groups of birds. Stonechats singing in the distance.

### 46 Woodlark
Song of a male; Nightjar singing a little way off.

### 47 Little Owl
Song of a male. With Woodlark and Nightjar continuing.

### 48 Nightjar, Robin
Song and calls of Nightjar. 'Tic' alarm calls from several Robins.

### 49 Dartford Warbler
Song of a male. With Nightjar, Stonechat and the soft, deep whinny of a horse in the background.

### 50 Stonechat
Songs of several males: Stonechats often breed in groups.

### 51 Hobby, Stonechat
Alarm calls of a male Hobby; various alarm calls from the Stonechats and a kind of distraction song.

### 52 Dartford Warbler
Alarm calls of 2 birds.

### 53 Tree Pipit
Song of a male in flight and perched.

### 54 LOWLAND WOODS Spring (13'08")
Like gardens and villages, woodlands can be a confusing mass of songs and calls; but the open, resonant acoustic makes it a wonderful place to

listen to bird song. The voices of woodland birds and the form of their songs have evolved in the context of the acoustics of woodland; it has been found that in general woodland birds tend more to purer tones and lower pitched songs than birds of open habitats. Remember that many of the species occuring in gardens and parks are generally common in woodlands.

## 54 Woodcock
Songflight of male. With Robins and Blackbirds singing.

## 55 Golden Oriole
Song of male. With Wren beginning to sing and Pheasant,

## 56 Pheasant
Display calls of several males; the screeching call is unusual. With Wood Pigeon singing.

## 57 Jay
Typical harsh calls.

## 58 Robin, Tawny Owl, Song Thrush
Alarm 'tic's from a Robin (and the soft clucks of a Pheasant); song of a male Tawny Owl; alarm call of a Song Thrush; calls of a female Tawny Owl with a Blue Tit beginning to sing assiduously.

## 59 Great Spotted Woodpecker
Drumming of several birds: the sound is made by a bird hammering its bill against the trunk or branch of a tree and is the equivalent of song. With a Wren song quite close and the trilling song of a Nuthatch.

## 60 Lesser Spotted Woodpecker
Drumming of several birds.

## 61 Nuthatch
Trilling song of the Nuthatch; a Blue Tit begins singing; typical calls from the Nuthatch; another frequently heard type of song from the Nuthatch. With Wren and Wood Pigeon in the background.

## 62 Blue Tit
Churring alarm calls. With alarm 'tic's from a Robin and a Blackcap singing in the Background.

## 63 Great Tit
Churring alarm calls and other calls probably signifying alarm. With several Wood Pigeons singing.

## 64 Marsh Tit
Contact calls; songs of the male; then song of a male Great Tit. With Bullfinch calls and song in the background.

## 65 Bullfinch
Contact or alarm calls; subsong from a male. With Great Tit continuing singing.

## 66 Willow Tit
Song. With Great Spotted Woodpecker drumming further off.

## 67 Chiffchaff
Song and call. With the very high-pitched, trilling calls of some Tree-creepers further off; and a Chaffinch beginning to sing in subsong.

## 68 Chaffinch
Subsong, probably from a young male beginning his first breeding season.

## 69 Fieldfare
Calls of one of several birds.

## 70 Stock Dove
Song of a male.

## 71 Hawfinch
Song, including variations on call notes.

## 72 WESTERN OAKWOOD Spring (8'15")
Depending on the distance North, many birds of lowland broad-leaved woods are also found in the western oakwoods; but a few species are more characteristic of the wet oakwoods (often with some birch) on the hillsides of upland areas, notably the Pied Flycatcher. Redstarts and Wood Warblers can be abundant; listen also for Tree Pipits.

## 72 Pied Flycatcher
Song of a male. With several Redstarts and a Wren singing further off.

## 73 Raven
Calls from a pair in flight.

## 74 Long-tailed Tit
Calls from a small party. With Pied Flycatcher and Willow Warbler further off.

## 75 Green Woodpecker, Treecreeper
Calls of a Green Woodpecker - the bird calls a second time around 10 seconds later; soft contact calls and song of a Treecreeper.

## 76 Wren
2 types of alarm call. With Redstart singing.

## 77 Redstart
Song and call.

## 78 Willow Warbler
Alarm (probably) and contact calls from several birds.

## 79 Sparrowhawk
Yikkering call, usually attributed to male (sex not confirmed here).

## 80 Cuckoo
Song and calls of 2 males, call of a female.

## 81 Willow Warbler
Song of a male, while moving through trees feeding.

## 82 Wood Warbler
Song of a male. With Chaffinch singing further off.

## 83 Spotted Flycatcher
Calls and song or subsong. With Wood Warbler and Curlew in the background.

## 84 Wood Warbler
Call and song.

## 85 NORTHERN PINEWOOD Spring (11'00")
Mature pinewoods, with spaced trees, have a wonderful acoustic, generally softer than broad-leaved woodland; supporting fewer total numbers of birds, and with fewer species, they make a good place to study bird song. In winter they can be very silent places, apart from the occasional flock of passerines; but in Spring the bird population swells and spreads out. As well as the species given here, Chaffinches, Blue and Great Tits, Robins, Willow Warblers, Woodcock and Tawny Owls are usually common; depending on the locality, Redstarts, Spotted Flycatchers and Tree Pipits may be quite common.

## 85 Capercaillie
Song or display calls of the male at lek. With Robin singing close by.

**86 Siskin**
Calls and song from perched male.

**87 Capercaillie**
Song or display calls of the male (close). With Siskin and Crested Tit in the vicinity.

**88 Crossbill**
Calls of several birds in a small party.

**89 Crested Tit**
Call or song - I'm not sure. With Goldcrest singing near.

**90 Mistle Thrush**
Song of a male.

**91 Goldcrest**
Calls and song. With Mistle Thrush and Coal Tits.

**92 Redpoll**
Song in flight from several birds; perched song from a single bird; calls and flight calls.

**93 Song Thrush**
Song of a male. With Wren singing.

**94 Buzzard**
Calls from a single bird.

**95 Black Grouse, Wren**
Song and display calls from several males at a Black Grouse lek; song of a male Wren. With Curlew singing in the distance and a Red Grouse at one point. A Chaffinch begins singing close by.

**96 Redwing**
Song of a male. With Chaffinch, Treecreeper, Black Grouse and Curlew.

**97 Coal Tit**
Song and calls from several birds. With Chaffinch and Wren.

# DISC 2

## 01 MOORLAND Spring (10'33")

We tend to use 'moorland' as a blanket term to cover a variety of open upland habitats, including grasslands and heaths, especially those dominated by heathers. Generally quiet in Winter, apart from occasional Red Grouse calls and displays in finer weather, from the early Spring there is an influx of waders and Meadow Pipits, followed by the migrants from abroad. Meadow Pipits and Skylarks are generally the most abundant passerines, both of which display with songflights; where there are groups of trees, a few woodland birds may crop up, especially the Willow Warbler. With the open aspect of this country, calls signifying various degrees of alarm are frequent as you pass through the breeding territories of various pairs of birds.

### 01 Lapwing
Display calls of several birds in flight; the rhythmic, heavy wingbeats are part of the display. Some Red Grouse calls from the moor. With Skylark and Curlew beginning to sing.

### 02 Curlew
Song and calls from several birds displaying in the air. With a Winchat beginning to sing nearby.

### 03 Winchat
Song of a male. With Curlews continuing to sing, then Red Grouse calling.

### 04 Winchat
Alarm calls.

### 05 Red Grouse
Display calls. With flight and other calls from some Meadow Pipits.

### 06 Meadow Pipit
Song flight of a male. With Red Grouse continuing to call.

### 07 Meadow Pipit, Black-headed Gull
Alarm calls from a pair with a nest nearby. Scolding calls from a Black-headed Gull and Red Grouse calls; then another Meadow Pipit song flight.

### 08 Ring Ouzel
Song of a male. With Wren and Meadow Pipit in the background.

### 09 Peregrine Falcon, Ring Ouzel
Alarm calls from a Peregrine Falcon; then alarm calls from the Ring Ouzel.

### 10 Wheatear
Alarm calls then song from a male. With a Skylark singing further off.

### 11 Ptarmigan
Calls from several birds taking flight. The Wheatear continues singing, then a dispute ensues with a second male.

### 12 FLOW COUNTRY Late Spring (8'50")
The moorlands to the North and West tend to wet upland peat-bogs and provide the breeding grounds for a variety of waders and other water birds, including divers. In more sheltered low-lying spots, traditional farming practises provide good habitats for a few more restricted species like the Twite. The herb-rich meadows on blown shell sand on the North-West seaboard, known as machairs, are proving a last refuge for the Corncrake in this region, as well as providing for an abundance of more widespread birds. The open moorland is often a silent place apart from the wind; but from spring into summer, on calmer and bright days, haunting sounds can be heard into the distance. Meadow Pipits and Skylarks are still generally the most abundant species.

### 12 Corncrake
Song of male; followed by song from several males in a densely-populated community. Then Skylark singing, Red Grouse (generally quite local in this habitat), Golden Plover and the snorting flight call of a Snipe on the edge of the flows.

### 13 Dunlin
Song and calls; then a Golden Plover song and some wails from a Red-throated Diver.

### 14 Golden Plover
Calls and song. With Skylark singing in the distance.

### 15 Red-throated Diver, Dunlin
Flight calls from a single Red-throat; various calls from Dunlin.

### 16 Greenshank
Sound of wings on a steep flight in; calls and song from several birds. With more Red-throat activity.

## 17 Red-throated Diver
Display calls and flight calls of 2 pairs.

## 18 Golden Plover
Song and display calls from several birds. Then calls from a flock of Twite and a passing Raven.

## 19 Raven, Twite
Calls from several birds in a flock of Twite; calls of a Raven in flight; calls from some individual Twite, then flight calls. With a Skylark singing in the background.

## 20 Redshank
Song and some calls. With several Golden Plover songs and calls.

## 21 WETLANDS Spring (11'08")
Lowland wetlands, with a mixture of marsh, reedbeds, open water and scrub or swampy woodland, can be densely packed with birds of the various species restricted to such habitats as well as those more typical of other habitats who manage to make a life here. There can be much to listen for through the Winter: Bearded Tits are at their most vocal in the Autumn and there may be migrant waders about. On early mornings in May and June the reedbeds can generate a wall of sound with the addition of the migrant warblers.

## 21 Nightingale
Song of a male from a Willow bush on the edge of a reedbed. With Yellowhammers singing in the distance; then a Sedge Warbler starting to sing.

## 22 Sedge Warbler, Reed Warbler
Sedge and Reed Warblers singing a little way off at the same time - or is it a Sedge imitating a Reed Warbler?

## 23 Reed Warbler
Song close by. With Sedge Warbler in the background.

## 24 Bittern
Song of a male. With Reed Warbler close and Sedge Warbler further off; some Greylag Goose calls, the calls of Bearded Tits, Cuckoo song and a Moorhen call

## 25 Bearded Tit, Bittern
Calls from a small party (4 or 5 birds); and the Bittern singing again. With Wren, Moorhen, Turtle Dove and Sedge Warbler.

### 26 Garganey
Display call of a drake - calls again a little later. With Sedge Warbler and Turtle Dove singing.

### 27 Sedge Warbler
Song of a male.

### 28 Grasshopper Warbler, Reed Bunting
Songs of males a little way off. This is a 3-note song from the Reed Bunting - cf 34 for a 4-note song.

### 29 Turtle Dove
Song of a male. With Grasshopper Warbler and Reed Bunting.

### 30 Water Rail
Song of a female. With Grasshopper Warbler.

### 31 Greylag Goose
Calls from one or both of a pair flying over.

### 32 Reed Bunting
Call of an individual. With Water Rail song and calls.

### 33 Grasshopper Warbler
Song of a male close by. With Water Rail calls and a Sedge Warbler alarm call.

### 34 Reed Bunting
Song of a male close by. With Grasshopper Warbler and Sedge Warbler songs and Water Rail calls.

### 35 Water Rail
Display calls - known as sharming. Display sounds, known as drumming, from a Snipe(cf 57).

### 36 Snipe
Breeding calls from several birds. With a buzzing alarm call from a Sedge Warbler.

### 37 LAKES & PONDS Spring (10'25")
The calls of the waterfowl, especially Coot and Moorhen, are typical of open freshwater pools; and the waterside vegetation, marsh, reedbed or woodland, determines the song birds in the vicinity. As well as the species mentioned here, various wagtails and warblers are also frequently found in waterside habitats; if there are muddy or gravely margins, there may be some waders about.

## 38 Canada Goose
Calls from several birds in a small flock. With Coot and Little Grebe calling.

## 39 Grey Heron
Calls of several birds from some nests in the wood by the pool.

## 40 Coot
Contact calls of an individual.

## 41 Teal
Calls of a drake. With a Blue Tit singing nearby.

## 42 Little Grebe
Call of a Moorhen; then display calls from a pair of Little Grebes.

## 43 Moorhen
Various loud and soft calls from several Moorhens. With Wren, Blue Tit, Song Thrush and Grey Heron further off.

## 44 Little Grebe
Display calls from several birds.

## 45 Great Crested Grebe
Display calls. With Wren, Wood Pigeon and Green Woodpecker further off. Then calls from several Coots disputing their areas and Willow Warblers beginning to sing.

## 46 Mallard
Call of a drake a little way off; then call of a female in flight.

## 47 Coot
'Kowp' calls from one bird. With a Stock Dove's song just audible in the distance.

## 48 Mallard
Calls of the males close by; followed by calls from several females - I usually refer to this as the 'laughing' call because it sounds like a laugh, not because I think the birds are laughing.

## 49 Coot
'Kowp' and 'pit' calls from a Coot.

## 50 Whooper Swan
Calls from a small flock heading North. With calls from a flock of Jackdaws and Wren and Willow Warblers still singing.

### 51 Coot
Softer 'kowp's and high 'zeet' calls.

### 52 Shoveler
Display calls of several drakes. With a Mistle Thrush singing in the distance.

### 53 Tufted Duck
Growling calls of a female; and display calls from some males.

### 54 RIVERS Spring (7'46")
As with lakes and ponds, many species we tend to regard as more typical of other habitats are found by rivers, depending on the nature of the land bordering the river. In general Kingfishers tend to be found on the slower flowing rivers and streams of the lowlands and the Dipper on the swifter waters of the uplands. Common Sandpipers are only common on the more northerly waters of the uplands; and Oystercatchers prefer waters with shingle-beds and riverside pastures, more typical of upland areas.

### 55 Sand Martin
Calls and snatches of song from several birds in the vicinity of a nesting colony. With Yellowhammer and Willow Warbler in the background.

### 56 Kingfisher
Calls of one bird. With Sand Martins calling and a Snipe 'drumming'.

### 57 Snipe
'Drumming' from a Snipe in display flight: the sound is produced by beating air over the outer tail feathers in a diving flight. With Sand Martins still calling nearby and the sneeze of a cow.

### 58 Kingfisher
Calls of one bird in flight. With a Robin singing from the bankside trees.

### 59 Grey Heron
Flight calls of a single bird. With Robin, Goldcrest and Great Tit nearby.

### 60 Dipper
Calls and then song from one bird, on a streamy section.

### 61 Grey Wagtail
Various calls/song from a male; including versions of the flight call,

though here delivered from a perched bird. With Wren and Common Sandpiper alarm calls and a Willow Warbler singing nearby.

### 62 Common Sandpiper
Calls or song from one bird. With calls from an Oystercatcher and the cough of a sheep.

### 63 Common Gull
Various calls, including the full display call, from several birds in a small flock.

### 64 Common Sandpiper, Oystercatcher
The Common Sandpiper begins singing the more usual type of song, before 3 Oystercatchers start calling on an aerial chase.

### 65 SUMMER SHORE (8'38")
The total numbers of birds on most stretches of coastline are probably less in Summer than Winter, but the terns are welcome summer breeders. Many of the species which winter on the coast, like the Curlew, Oystercatcher or the gulls, move to upland areas or quieter northern coasts to breed in the Spring; but there are often a few individuals of even these species to be seen throughout the Summer - some juveniles, non-breeders and local breeders come to feed. This piece begins in a small fishing village harbour, then moves near quite a rocky headland protecting a small muddy inlet with sandy shingle along the tide-line.

### 65 Eider Duck
Calls of a female Eider, harried by a Herring Gull. Some of the larger gulls frequently hang around the harbour wall and attack the Eiders when they surface from a dive. With House Sparrows and Starlings calling from the surrounding buildings.

### 66 Great Black-backed Gull
Long display call from the harbour wall, with the Eiders still calling in agitation. Followed by softer mewings, mostly from the Herring Gulls I think.

### 67 Herring Gull
Long display call; and various softer calls.

### 68 Sandwich Tern
Calls of a bird flying a little way off-shore. With the display call of a Herring Gull in the distance and the deep 'kaow' of a Great Black-backed closer by.

## 69 Common Tern
Calls of several birds, who join in a chase.

## 70 Great Black-backed Gull
'Kaow' calls from one bird at an intruder - me.

## 71 Lesser Black-backed Gull
'Kaow' calls from quite a party of birds come to investigate the threat.

## 72 Herring Gull, Oystercatcher
Calls of one bird at the intruder. The calls of an Oystercatcher arriving, probably to feed.

## 73 Ringed Plover, Dunlin
Calls and song from several Ringed Plover and Dunlin courting around the tide-line. This remains for me a fascinating account of something I couldn't quite see at the time because of a clump of heather. I think a pair of Ringed Plover are trying out nest hollows and are joined by a third bird at some point. Later there are calls from a Common Gull, Sandwich Terns and Arctic Terns.

## 74 Arctic Tern
Various calls from several birds in a party, including the rhythmic, stuttering calls which accompany the kind of display-chase terns indulge in - presumably their equivalent of song. Aggressive calls accompanying dive-bombing attacks.

## 75 Whimbrel
Calls of a single bird flying past.

## 76 Mute Swan
The wing-beats of a pair flying over. Distant calls from a Curlew.

## 77 WINTER SALTMARSH (8'22")
Saltmarshes and mudflats can be busy with bird life in the Winter as many more northerly or inland breeders gather for the rich feeding. Just before and just after high tide many birds tend to be on the move in small flocks between feeding and roosting areas and can be quite vocal.

## 77 Curlew
Calls of several birds.

## 78 Redshank
Calls of several birds feeding on a creek nearby.

## 79 Pink-footed Goose
Calls of a single bird flying by.

## 80 Brent Goose
Calls from a small flock a little way off.

## 81 Shelduck
Display calls from males and females. With the thin piping call of a Dunnock in the bushes nearby.

## 82 Skylark
Calls from one or two birds flying past. With Shelduck calls.

## 83 White-fronted Goose
Calls from a small flock flying past.

## 84 Wigeon
Display calls of males in a small flock in the distance.

## 85 Oystercatcher
Calls of a bird arriving to feed. With some Wigeon calling closer.

## 86 Bewick's Swan
Flight calls from a small flock. With Wigeon and Redshank calls.

## 87 Redshank
Calls of several birds. With some Robin song and calls from the bushes.

## 88 Teal, Black-headed Gull
Display calls of a male Teal. With display calls from several Black-headed Gulls and the wing-beats of a small flock of Wigeon passing.

## 89 Wigeon
Growling quacks of female taking flight.

## 90 Teal
Call of female. With Redshanks calling and Robin, Dunnock and Wren in the nearby bushes.

## 91 SEACLIFF Early Summer (6'42")
Densely-packed breeding space involves much social interaction and sea-bird colonies can be raucous places as display and disputes pass through different areas. There are usually a good number of Kittiwakes and they are rarely silent. The sound of a disturbed colony in full clamour makes an acoustic hell for most people - an effective deterrent to intruders.

## 91 Kittiwake
Various calls from many birds, in flight and perched - 'kittiwaak's, 'kow's and various moans and mewings. With some Fulmar and Guillemot calls later.

## 92 Guillemot
Display and aggressive calls from several birds. With some calls from one of several Jackdaws moving around the ledges. More Guillemot calls, with Kittiwakes wheeling and calling.

## 93 Razorbill
Display calls. With Kittiwake and later some Guillemot calls.

## 94 Fulmar
Display calls from several pairs on nearby ledges. With Rock Pipit calls.

## 95 Rock Pipit
Various calls and song in display flight from several birds.

## 96 Chough
Calls from one of two birds passing over.

## 97 Eider
Display calls of drakes; with some female calls later.

# SPECIES ACCOUNTS

Species are given in systematic order in the account: this can be quite intriguing in relation to bird vocalisation. Different species within a genus, and in some cases related genera, as might be expected, often share similar vocal characteristics - pigeons coo, waders often pipe or whistle and warblers usually have warbling songs and churring alarm calls. Also there are good evolutionary reasons why some particular types of call might be similar in different species: alarm calls used by scolding birds tend to be harsh or piercing, unpleasant to the ears of the intruder as well as drawing attention to him. Where species flock together or habitually associate, there may be communicative advantages to having similar types of call for similar situations. But evolutionary pressure also works the other way, when species identity is important to the communication, as is the case with song; a singing male needs to attract a female of his own species and not waste energy singing in contest with males of other species. So closely related species, often visually very similar, as in the Chiffchaff and the Willow Warbler, the Chaffinch and the Brambling, have usually evolved with quite distinct forms of song.

## DIVERS - GAVIIDAE

Rarely heard during the winter months which they generally spend at sea, the divers become much more vociferous on their breeding grounds in spring. Their vocabulary ranges from fairly pure-toned wailing sounds to harsh croaks, generally audible up to 1 km away, inreasonable conditions.

**Red-throated Diver**   *Gavia stellata*                          2,15; 2,17
The Red-throat's wail is a drawn-out mewing note, with a slight pitch slide, given by both male and female. Generally part of courtship and territorial displays, it may also be given when a predator flies over. A harsh cackling duet is also part of courtship (2,17). These cries are accompanied by ritual posturing with the long neck and bill. A harsh quack, often repeated in series, is given by birds in flight (2,15); sometimes the courtship cackle is given in flight. Birds return to their breeding grounds on moorland lochans in April and May.

**Black-throated Diver**   *Gavia arctica*
The usual wail of the Black-throat has a similar tone to the Red-throat, but has a distinct, yodelling motif to it. This may be accompanied by

eerie lower-pitched wails in display. Other calls frequently heard are dog-like, sharp yelps and Raven-like, deep croaks, which may be given in flight. Moves into its breeding areas on larger upland lochs in April and May.

### Great Northern Diver   *Gavia immer*

This diver has similar wailing cries to the Black-throat, with a wider range of motifs, notably a kind of laughing, ululating cry (frequently heard setting the atmosphere on North American wilderness films). Also gives a barking quack in flight.

## GREBES - PODICIPEDIDAE

The calls of the grebes show affinities with both the divers and the species higher in the systematic order: the tubenoses, geese and ducks, both in vocal timbre and the form of the calls. Ranging from the shrill notes of the Little, Slavonian and Black-necked Grebes, with a hint of the divers' wailing cries, to the harsher croaking of the Great-crested and Red-necked, occasionally hinting at the divers and the tubenoses.

### Little Grebe   *Tachybaptus ruficollis*   2,42;2,44

The most frequently heard sound of the Little Grebe is the shrill, rapid trilling display song, usually given as a duet; this might be confused with the bubbling call of a female Cuckoo (1,80). Though most frequent in spring, it can be heard at other times. A brief descending trill call, similar to the display song, is frequently heard through the summer, as is a sharp peeping from anxious birds.

### Great Crested Grebe   *Podiceps cristatus*   2,45

A rough, diver-like, croaking voice is the mark of the Great Crested Grebe. Frequently heard in display on the water in Spring, their calls range from staccato chakk's to harder, braying quacks and rough, purring growls. Usually calls are repeated in a series. Can sound rather like a duck species' quack or a Grey Heron's 'kraak' on occasions.

### Red-necked Grebe   *Podiceps grisegena*

Calls with an elongated croaky bray and a rapid 'keck-keck-keck...'. Quite like a rough-voiced Mallard. These sounds are also used in display.

### Slavonian Grebe   *Podiceps auritus*

The Slavonian calls with a thin, short mew, quite gull-like. In display, this is lengthened to a laughing trill, with a distinct end note and often a cawing tone. Many variations on this theme can be heard, often mixed with repeated single note calls.

**Black-necked Grebe** *Podiceps nigricollis*
The Black-necked Grebe calls with a squeaky 'pweee-pe' or sharper 'peep' note, often repeated. In territorial and courtship display, birds produce chattering sequences in a similar voice to the calls. Also said to give crooning calls.

## TUBENOSES - PROCELLARIIDAE

When they are at sea, the tubenoses are fairly solitary birds and the species covered here are rarely heard to give voice. Courtship and breeding, which take place on land, are a different matter: the birds become very vocal, with various crooning, churring and cackling calls being a mark of the family.

**Fulmar** *Fulmarus glacialis*                                                2,94
Usually silent in flight, the Fulmar occasionally gives a soft, snorty 'cough'. Birds become very vocal in display on their breeding ledges and in greetings when a paired bird returns to its mate. They sing with harsh cackles and chuckles, subsiding into prolonged gutteral, crooning purrs. Often birds are found at the breeding ledges through the winter; but the presence of a few birds displaying at a site is not necessarily a sign of breeding; they may be young birds prospecting a possible breeding site.

**Manx Shearwater** *Puffinus puffinus*
Manx Shearwaters become vociferous around their breeding colonies at night when adults come in off the sea. Flying in after dark, the birds call repeatedly with variations on a 2 or 3 note cawing (or crowing) cry, followed by a wheezy croon (the croon as if on the intake of breath): 'cacoocoo-ooo'. More adults visit their nests on overcast nights than clear ones and at large colonies the air can be filled by the raucous clamour of thousands of unseen birds. Adults also cackle and croon in their nesting burrows, sometimes for long periods.

## PETRELS - HYDROBATIDAE

**Storm Petrel** *Hydrobates pelagicus*
At night in their breeding haunts and their nesting burrows, pairs become very vocal. They sing a purring, crooning song for long spells without interruption. The theme is a slightly shrill churr, rising in pitch

to a croaky note, repeated over and over. Birds also give soft, shrill squelching calls.

**Leach's Petrel**   *Oceanodroma leucorhoa*
Leach's Petrels purr in a similar way to the Storm Petrel, but interspersed with short wheezes and little, squealing 'ooh's, rising quickly in pitch. More distinctive is a fast, staccato, 'laughing' motif, very reminiscent of the cartoon character Woody Woodpecker's signature call. These calls are part of the birds' breeding displays and are only heard during their nocturnal visits to their breeding sites on remote islands.

## GANNETS - SULIDAE

**Gannet**   *Sula bassana*
Like the tubenoses, Gannets are rarely heard at sea, but in courtship, greetings between pairs and status disputes at their breeding colonies, they become vociferous. They honk and croak to each other in a deep, hoarse, gutteral voice, repeating short calls with variations in rhythm and pitch.

## CORMORANTS - PHALACROCORACIDAE

**Cormorant**   *Phalacrocorax carbo*
Although individuals tend to hunt alone, cormorants are fairly social and frequently gather to preen, dry their wings and roost; but these gatherings are often quiet affairs. At their breeding colonies Cormorants become much more vocal. In display, they produce gutteral, crooning croaks with various rhythmic motifs. Nesting birds challenge intruders with harsh, throaty grunts and clicks.

**Shag**   *Phalacrocorax aristotelis*
Shags have a similar voice to their close relative, the Cormorant, and similar vocal behaviour. Nesting birds produce rasping grunts and clicks.

## HERONS - ARDEIDAE

**Bittern**   *Botaurus stellaris*                                2,24;2,25
The Bittern is one of those birds that has traditionally been best known for its distinct and unusual song. Male Bitterns sing in display from their dense reed-bed territories, producing sequences of deep, hollow 'booming' notes, that can be heard a kilometre away in good conditions. Often individual males can be distinguished by the form of their boom by ear;

recent research, using computers to look more closely at the frequency pattern, has provided a finer discrimination and enabled the individual identification of probably all the males calling in Britain. Booming can be heard in settled weather from the early spring (February) through to the Summer. Beware of bulls producing a subdued, breathy bellowing which can carry far on a still morning. In flight birds sometimes give a harsh 'kwaa'.

**Grey Heron**   *Ardea cinerea*                               2,39;2,59
Grey Herons are often heard calling a harsh 'kraank', usually repeated a few times at invervals, in flight, sometimes scolding an intruder (2,59); the actual call shows a little variation in voicing between birds. Various harsh yells and shrieks are heard around nesting colonies, often as a bird is returning to the site, and clattering runs of bill-clicking in display at the nest (2,39). Breeding begins early and colonies can be very noisy in February.

## SWANS, GEESE AND DUCKS - ANATIDAE

Whereas the previous families of birds can be characterised by a tendency towards gutteral sounding voices, the species of this family tend towards voices of a nasal timbre. They are also prone to be more vocal in general than the previous families outside the breeding season, usually spending the rest of the year in more coherent social groups - anything from pairs or smaller family parties to massive flocks. Flocking activity can become very noisy as many birds call at once, particularly around take-off, landing and meetings with other flocks.

**Mute Swan**   *Cygnus olor*                               2,76
Usually silent birds, Mute Swans often hiss or grunt softly to threaten an intruder. They also call occasionally when displaying, with quite musical squeals or mews, but possibly their most frequently-heard sound is the whistle of their heavy wing-beats (2,76).

**Bewick's Swan**   *Cygnus columbianus*                     2,86
Quite vocal birds, Bewicks converse with each other with tonally quite pure hoops and honks. These vary from soft, lower-pitched 'hoo's of feeding birds to the louder, higher-pitched, more shrill honking, with various rhythmic motifs, in flocking activities.

**Whooper Swan**   *Cygnus cygnus*                           2,50
Like the Bewick's Swan, the Whooper calls frequently and with a similar kind of vocalisation to its relative. But its voice is generally lower-

pitched, more croaky and at times with the timbre of a bugle or trumpet. Despite their rather limited vocal range, Whoopers produce a wide variety of sounds and motifs.

**Bean Goose**   *Anser fabalis*
Possibly less vocal than the other grey geese, Bean Geese have nonetheless a similar variety of calls. In flight, calls are a rough honk, often given in quick runs of two or three, 'arr-arr-arr' or the traditional rendition 'ung-unk'. Individuals also give a variety of calls in other circumstances, from shrill squeals to harsh barks and strange nasal honks.

**Pink-footed Goose**   *Anser brachyrhynchus*                      2,79
A very vocal bird, but with a flight call that is hoarser than that of White-fronted Geese. In a flock they become more excited with shrill variations - the usual rendering is 'wink,wink'. Other calls range from soft, shivering croaks and squeaks, to more strident sqeeling honks. Think 'barking'.

**White-fronted Goose**   *Anser albifrons*                        2,83
Voice and vocal behaviour are broadly similar to the Pink-footed Goose: flight calls tend to a yapping squeal, given in rippling runs. Other calls are soft gabbles, similar to the Pinkfoot, but with less tonal variation - something of a yapping honk. Lesser Whitefronts' voices tend to a higher pitch. Think 'yapping'.

**Greylag Goose**   *Anser anser*                                  2,31
The Greylag's calls have a distinct nasal timbre. Flight calls range from deep rough barks, to more open honks; these can be emphatically monosyllabic, but frequently have rhythmic accentuation, producing various whinnying or gabbling motifs. Vocally similar to its domesticated descendants, farmyard geese.

**Canada Goose**   *Branta canadensis*                             2,38
Canada Geese have a relatively deep, slightly hoarse voice. They call frequently with a repeated brief, coarse honk, ending in a quick rise in pitch to a shriller note; also with a more drawn-out, bugle like 'aah-', often ending in the squeaky honk. Flight calls also include similar zipping honks, tending to sound more like a single syllable.

**Barnacle Goose**   *Branta leucopsis*
Feeding Barnacle Geese call with repeated, soft yaps. In other situations, birds produce more strident, short yapping honks 'how, how', which may rise to Jackdaw-like yelps, and sometimes low, groaning honks.

**Brent Goose**   *Branta bernicla*                                    2,80
The Brent's voice (like the Barnacle) is less strident than the other geese.
Birds call with purring 'rrurr's and more abrupt 'rruk's, repeated with
variations in rhythm and pitch. Calls from a large flock merge into one
rolling groan.

*Ducks*

All the ducks have quacking calls, that differ to some extent in timbre
and rhythm of calling. | In some species the female's quack is closer to a
growl. Distinguishing species is not easy, but useful for marking the
presence of a hidden bird. The drakes of many species also have
whistling calls which they give in display, varying from the high-pitched,
thin, wheezing performance of the Shelduck to the single note bleat of
the Teal and the explosive wheeze of the Shoveler.

**Shelduck**   *Tadorna tadorna*                                      2,81
Quite a vocal bird, the Shelduck's vocal displays can be heard at almost
any time of year, but probably most frequently through the winter and
spring. In display the males produce an accelerating series of wizzy
whistles (more varied and wheezing than a drake Wigeon); this is often
accompanied by a rapidly-repeated, gutteral ack-ack-ack..., possibly
from the females, which may become more of a churr. Birds also give a
rising, ratchety quack call.

**Mandarin**   *Aix galericulata*
Generally quiet birds, the male sometimes gives a sharp whistle in flight
and the female a quacking 'aak'.

**Wigeon**   *Anas penelope*                                      2,84;2,89
The drake Wigeon's distinctive display call is a whistled 'whee-yoo', the
'whee' rising sharply in pitch and the 'yoo' at a lower pitch (2,84).
Flocks can become vociferous as the males indulge in this display
whistling. The female is most often heard to give a gutteral, croaky
quack (with a hint of a corvid), usually repeated and often in flight
(2,89).

**Gadwall**   *Anas strepera*
Difficult to distinguish vocally from the Mallard, the female Gadwall's
quack seems higher-pitched, often given in series. The male has a
slightly harsher and thinner quack than a Mallard, with a slightly nasal
tone, accompanied by whistles in display.

**Teal**  *Anas crecca*  2,41;2,88;2,90
The drake Teal's display call is a high, clear, bell-like bleep, often referred to as a 'bleat' (2,41;2,88), heard all year round. The female's quack is high-pitched, thin and raspy (2,90). Birds also give a chattering 'krik' call.

**Mallard**  *Anas platyrhynchos*  2,46;2,48
Female Mallards produce classic single quacks, with a slightly raspy timbre and a rising pitch; they also utter runs of quacks, like laughing, descending in pitch and intensity. Males produce softer, lower-pitched quacks, with a bubbling, or even grating quality, and a soft whistle in display.

**Pintail**  *Anas acuta*
Pintail drakes produce a high-pitched bleating, 'prup', rather like a drake Teal, with a wheezing undertone. This is often accompanied by soft, chuckling quacks in a slightly hoarse voice from the females. Females also produce full, loud quacks like female Mallards, but slightly thinner and higher-pitched.

**Garganey**  *Anas querquedula*  2,26
Females have a thin, lamb-like quack; males have a very distinct, rattling call, like a card run slowly and erratically along a comb. Displaying birds also produce thin, chittering quacks.

**Shoveler**  *Anas clypeata*  2,52
Shoveler drakes produce soft, wheezing, often double phuts in court-ship, 'huk-huk', the second usually lower-pitched than the first. Females have a thin, hoarse, high-pitched quack.

**Pochard**  *Aythya ferina*
In flight, female Pochard produce a repeated, churring growl, 'rrurr'; displaying males produce rising, flutey wheezes and sometimes Eider-like croons. Birds also utter thin, scratchy quacks.

**Tufted Duck**  *Aythya fuligula*  2,53
Tufted Duck, mostly fairly quiet, can become quite vocal at times. Males produce soft, rippling 'laughs' in a wheezing voice in courtship and status displays. Females give quite a harsh, churring quack, often in flight, and gruff, barking quacks in display on the water.

**Scaup**  *Aythya marila*
Scaup are rarely heard; but they produce low, gruff growls and higher

barking growls, that can hardly be described as quacks. Displaying males sing with a wheezing 'a-whew', accent on the second syllable.

**Eider**  *Somateria mollissima*                                    2,65;2,97
Eider drakes in display sing with short, quite deep, crooning notes like 'oooh', sometimes a disyllabic 'aa-ooh', loud enough to be heard at 200-300m. Each full call usually rises, then subsides in pitch (2,97). This is accompanied by soft, gruff quacking from the females; females also produce much louder, grating quacks when alarmed (2,65).

**Long-tailed Duck**  *Clangula hyemalis*
Drakes call with a yodelling half-honk, reminiscent of geese and quite tuneful though repetitive, accompanied by quacking 'uuh's possibly from the females. Display calls are frequently heard from birds in flocks, often with various crooning notes.

**Common Scoter**  *Melanitta nigra*
Displaying Common Scoter produce a rhythmic bleeping, reminiscent of the yikkering of a Common Snipe, but with a purer tone.

**Velvet Scoter**  *Melanitta fusca*
Displaying pairs call with terse, thin, repeated quacks. Females also give a querulous, rapid 'a-ha-ha-ha' quack.

**Goldeneye**  *Bucephala clangula*
The characteristic rapid whistling of its wing-beats is probably the most frequently heard sound of the Goldeneye. Males produce a very thin, nasal quack, and a fuller, disyllabic, ratchety call in display; females in flight repeat a lower-pitched, growling quack, similar to a Wigeon or Tufted female.

**Red-breasted Merganser**  *Mergus serrator*
Generally a quiet bird, the Red-breasted Merganser is sometimes heard to utter croaking quacks, often in cackling runs. Displaying males give quiet, wheezing croaks.

**Goosander**  *Mergus merganser*
Most often heard calling in flight with a short, repeated, gruff croak. Similar calls are occasionally heard in other situations. Displaying males produce a Fulmar-like cackling. Birds in autumn gatherings can become quite vocal, but not particularly loud.

## HAWKS & FALCONS - ACCIPITRIDAE

These families are not in general audibly vocal birds, other than when alarmed by an intruder, or calling occasionally in courtship display, the exception being the Buzzards. Nevertheless paired birds frequently communicate vocally, but generally in the vicinity of the nest and often with quieter calls. In many species, males bringing in prey to the nest call to the female, who then comes to take the food from them. Young birds can be vociferous, both in the nest and for a while after fledging. Voices are often thin and high-pitched for the size of bird; whistles, yelps, mewing, chittering and repeated 'kecking' calls characterise this group.

**Honey Buzzard**   *Pernis apivorus*
The Honey Buzzard's most distinctive calls are thin, plaintive whistles, which quickly rise, then gradually descend a little in pitch.

**Red Kite**   *Milvus milvus*
Red Kite calls are often similar in form to a Common Buzzard's mewing, but given as a whistle. They can sound like a Honey Buzzard, but with more variation and a variety of motifs, some sounding like wolf-whistles.

**White-tailed Eagle**   *Haliaeetus albicilla*
White-tailed Eagles' calls seem to be in one of two voices: a louder, repeated, thin, squealing yelp, often staccato, but sometimes lengthened; and a softer, gruff, croaking yelp, usually repeated. Both types of call are variable.

**Marsh Harrier**   *Circus aeruginosus*
Marsh Harriers are rarely vocal outside the breeding season. Males sometimes produce a thin, short yelp; birds call a rapid 'kek-kek-kek...' in alarm at an intruder.

**Hen Harrier**   *Circus cyaneus*
Hen Harriers can be quite vocal in aerial display, when the birds produce various squeals and chitterings. In alarm, birds call with a 'kek-kek-kek...', more rapid and higher-pitched than the Marsh Harrier.

**Montagu's Harrier**   *Circus pygargus*
In aerial displays Montagu's Harriers call with various soft squeals, 'chakk's and 'churr's. Their alarm call is similar to the other harriers, with something of a squeaking quality to it.

**Goshawk**   *Accipiter gentilis*
Goshawks rarely call away from the nest site. Adults produce full-sounding, squealing yelps, quite similar to some gull's calls and a 'kek-ing' like the other hawks, reminiscent of a slower, more strident yaffle from a Green Woodpecker.

**Sparrowhawk**   *Accipiter nisus*                                    1,79
Sparrowhawks call with a rapidly-repeated, quite shrill 'kew-kew-kew...' Males bringing in prey call to females on the nest, who then come to take the food from a nearby perch or plucking post.

**Buzzard**   *Buteo buteo*                                            1,94
Buzzards are generally more vocal than other hawks and falcons, or at least more often heard. Birds call in courtship, alarm, status and territorial disputes and other situations with variations on a mewing 'me-ooow', which has a sharp attack then trails off into the mew. These tend to be more abrupt and more shrill from an alarmed bird. Birds call most frequently in flight.

**Rough-legged Buzzard**   *Buteo lagopus*
Very similar calls to the Common Buzzard; possibly a slightly thinner sounding voice with more drawn-out calls.

**Golden Eagle**   *Aquila chrysaetos*
Wild Golden Eagles are rarely vocal away from the nest site; and even at the nest adults are usually silent. Their usual call is quite a thin, yelping 'kyaa' and variations. Young birds in the nest can be quite vocal prior to and after fledging.

## OSPREYS - PANDIONIDAE

**Osprey**   *Pandion haliaetus*
Ospreys call with a repeated, quite strident whistle, 'hew-hew-hew-hew....'. Birds also give a thin squeal in alarm.

## FALCONS - FALCONIDAE

**Kestrel**   *Falco tinnunculus*                                      1,11
Females call in the vicinity of the nest with a querulous, rippling 'quee-quee-quee...'. Birds are also frequently heard calling with a shrill, yikker-ing 'ke-ke-ke...', often on the wing. This is often heard from a family group in summer or from a bird being mobbed. In alarm the 'kek's become more drawn out and grating.

**Merlin**   *Falco columbarius*
Territorial and alarm calls are based on a shrill 'keking' similar in tone to
a Peregrine, but more rapid and higher-pitched.

**Hobby**   *Falco subbuteo*                                                        1,51
The Hobby's calls include a repeated, squealing 'yhew-yhew-yhew...'
with a hint of a whistle in the tone and a descending pitch to each
syllable. Squeals and clicks, similar to a Kestrel, but with a purer tone,
are also heard.

**Gyrfalcon**   *Falco rusticolus*
Calls in the vicinity of the nest site in a voice reminiscent of a Peregrine;
but the notes are more drawn out and not so harsh.

**Peregrine Falcon**   *Falco peregrinus*                                           2,9
Birds call readily in alarm at an intruder near the nest site with a hoarse,
grating 'keck-keck-keck...' (2,9). Softer, drawn-out squeals and chittering squeals are sometimes heard, generally around the nest site.

## GROUSE - TETRAONIDAE

The breeding systems of the grouse differ between the first two species,
of the Lagopus genus, birds of more open habitat, and the next two
species, woodland grouse of the Tetrao genus. The Lagopus males
defend a breeding and, to some extent, feeding territory in keeping with
a more or less promiscuous monogamy; in the polygamous system of
the Tetrao species, the male's status display has become more ritualised
and territory is replaced with a stance at the lek. Competition, involving
what have been called 'song substitutes', is for a higher status stance,
which seems to carry more right to mate with the attendant females (for
the males) and make its occupier more desirable to the females. At the
lek males sing for much of the time; calling, or the equivalent of singing,
is more sporadic with the Lagopus species males, but these tend to be
more vocal birds in other situations.

**Red (or Willow) Grouse**   *Lagopus lagopus*                                      2,5
Generally quite a vocal bird, which almost always calls when flushed or
taking flight. On fine days in Autumn and Spring displaying birds can
be very vocal for periods and a well-populated moor comes alive with
soft cackling in the distance, as birds make short crowing flights with the
occasional physical conflict. Generally calling is based on a rattling
cackle, gradually rising in pitch and speeding up, sometimes ending in
several single notes, followed by repeated, fairly rapid 'gobak's, said to

be warning you to 'go back'. Both the cackle and the 'gobak' may be given individually. Occasionally birds are heard to give softer, crooning calls in a similar tone of voice.

**Ptarmigan**   *Lagopus mutus*                                    2,11
In the windy silence of the mountain top or tundra, a deep, gutteral croak, resembling a human belch, is the clue that a well-camouflaged Ptarmigan is nearby. Birds almost always call before or when taking flight. Often a single note is given 'slowed down', then sounding like a dry rattle. The male has a territorial crowing song in the same voice, heard in Spring.

**Black Grouse**   *Tetrao tetrix*                                  1,95
Generally quiet and always wary, the males (known as blackcocks as opposed to the greyhens) become very vocal at the lek. At dawn and sometimes in the evening, the males gather at traditional sites for their lekking displays; odd birds can turn up at any season of the year, but late Winter through to Summer is the busiest period. Within their individual areas around 3 or 4 metres apart, the cocks make circling dances, usually with the head down and tail fanned out, and adopt various other postures competing for status. Occasionally a dispute breaks out with a vigorous beating of wings and hissing sneezes. The whole do is to the accompaniment of a chorus of bubbling or crooning, rather like a pigeon or dove. The full song is actually a stereotyped pattern of around four seconds in length. With different birds singing simultaneously, but out of phase with each other, the result is a chorus of bubbling. Though apparently soft, this bubbling can be heard a kilometre away on a calm morning. Birds have a particular call, heard at the lek and occasionally away from it, 'cucurricoohu' or some similar motif, in their crooning voice. Sometimes calls a quick, slightly yelping 'up-up-up' when taking flight, and a similar call is occasionally heard from females in other situations.

**Capercaillie**   *Tetrao urogallus*                          1,85;1,87
Like the Black Grouse, rarely heard to call away from the lek; occasion-ally birds of either sex give a terse, throaty 'kuk-kuk-kuk...' call. Males at the lek have more widely-spaced stances than Blackcock, from which they perform; it is more of an individual affair than the Black Grouse's. Males fan their tails, droop their wings, swell their iridescent green breasts and their red eyebrows and repeat their stereotyped song for several hours. Each song begins with a series of spaced double clicks, gradually accelerating to a clear, cork-from-the-bottle 'pop', followed by

a wheezing, frenetic warble. Each rendition usually lasts between 6 and 10 seconds, depending on the amount of introductory clicks. Display begins in the near-darkness of early dawn and is most frequent in April, but can take place any time in the Spring when conditions are favourable. Occasional 'rogue' males are prone to display at any time away from the lek and can even attack humans or vehicles; such birds are rare and tend to be reported in the press.

## PHEASANTS, PARTRIDGES & QUAIL - PHASIANIDAE

The calls of this family are generally based around crowing notes in a hoarse, often scratchy voice (the exception here is the Quail). Breeding is in a territorial system and males have simple, often quite loud, territorial calls accompanying displays.

**Red-legged Partridge**   *Alectoris rufa*                                1,38
Birds in a flock call with a wheezy squeal in flight. Displaying males call with sharp 'chuck's, building up to fuller display calls - rhythmic variations around scratchy 'chuck-chk-arr' motifs.

**Grey Partridge**   *Perdix perdix*                                        1,32
Territorial display call is a more stereotyped repetition than the Red-leg, consisting in an elongated scratchy note which often becomes a disyllabic 'chirrrr-ick'. This is usually given in runs of around half a dozen at intervals, which can be lengthy. Frequently heard around dusk and dawn, less so during the day. Territorial and courtship displays are often accompanied by short aerial chases and a sort of yikkering in a similar scratchy voice. Calls in a flock and in flight tend to be based on repeated, sharp 'tchik's, sometimes with the odd 'chirr-ick'.

**Quail**   *Coturnix coturnix*                                            1,37
The territorial and courtship call of the Quail is a repeated, whiplash-like, whistled triplet, often rendered 'wet-my-lips'. This call can be heard from nearly a kilometre away in calm conditions. Each series may be introduced by a soft wheezing sound, only audible from close by. As this is a small bird that usually remains hidden in the vegetation on its breeding grounds, this call is often the only indication of its presence.

**Pheasant**   *Phasianus colchicus*                                       1,56
Intermittently a very vocal bird, the Pheasant's calls are based on short, explosive crowing notes with a wheezing croak to them. Females are seldom heard. Displaying males usually stand with head held high on some prominence and give a loud, distinctly disyllabic 'kurr kuk', usu-

ally followed by a brief, but powerful and rapid beating of their wings; this is performed at variable intervals. Birds taking flight often give a repeated 'kurruk, kurruk...' to accompany the clatter of the rapid wing-beats. Birds going to roost often call a single 'kurk', repeated at short intervals, often with occasional variations. Also heard around a roost, if you are close to birds, is a soft mewing and clucking, some notes pleasant to the ear, some thin and squeaky. Vocal for most of the year.

**Golden Pheasant**   *Chrysolophus pictus*
The male's display call is a loud, squawky shriek, something like a Jay and usually given from dense cover; this is often accompanied by much softer musical cluckings.

## RAILS & CRAKES - RALLIDAE

**Water Rail**   *Rallus aquaticus*                                  2,30;2,35
Though apparently silent for much of the time, Water Rails can become very vocal in the breeding season. Calling is based on shrill, trilling squeals, which vary from short, explosive, repeated 'pip's to more elongated, wheezing or piercing squeals (2,30 - female call or song). Courtship and display involves a vocal performance known as 'sharm-ing' - a building series of calls incorporating squeals and groans like a stomach churning, frequently subsiding into softer runs of throaty clicks (2,35). The squealing calls can often be heard at a distance, but many of the sharming sounds can only be heard from nearby. Tends to be more vocal in the late evening, through the night and the early morning.

**Spotted Crake**   *Porzana porzana*
Like the Water Rail, more often heard than seen. In the breeding season males call with a strident, whistling 'whit', repeated at intervals of around a second or less, often for long periods. Usually heard from dusk into the night. Birds are also said to call with a rhythmic, snipe-like yikker. Birds are not often heard on their northern breeding grounds before June.

**Corncrake**   *Crex crex*                                          2,12
The Corncrake has some softer calls which are rarely heard. But the bird used to be well known in most farming areas in Northern Europe from the generally-nocturnal display calls of the males, whence it gets its scientific name 'crex crex'. The bursts of two ratchety notes are re-peated often endlessly, at short (less than 1 second) intervals; calling birds broadcast in all directions by slowly turning their heads, giving rise

to a reputed ventriloquial quality. Birds call most frequently between midnight and 3am, tending to prefer balmy nights, but the number of birds calling on any particular night is variable. The call can be heard from when the birds start to arrive in May, through to July. Birds of passage are often heard calling at potential breeding sites.

**Moorhen**   *Gallinula chloropus*                                           2,43
Generally quite a vocal bird, the most distinctive call of the Moorhen is a ringing 'prrrt', often given when disturbed. But it also has a wide vocabulary of other calls, varying from soft clucks to a strident 'chid' or 'chidou' and various 'hecks', similar to its close relative and often co-inhabitant, the Coot. Both birds are very vocal in territorial and status disputes, calling in similar patterns and at most times of the year. Other than recognising the diagnostic calls, distinguishing between the species is a matter of becoming familiar with differences in the timbre of their voices: Coot calls tend to begin with an explosive element 'k', whereas Moorhen calls seem to build from an aspiration into an explosive element 'huk'. Moorhens often call in runs of notes with distinct rhythmic motifs. Flushed birds often call with a loud, rhythmic run of 'kurruk's as they reach cover. Solitary pairs on a river are generally less vocal than pairs in close proximity at larger sites.

**Coot**   *Fulica atra*                                     2,40;2,47;2,49;2,51
Coots are generally very vocal birds throughout the year, probably more than Moorhens. Often tending to socially quite crowded breeding, territorial and status displays are frequent and vocal. Some of the most diagnostic sounds of the Coot are repeated, explosive, metallic 'phut's' and 'zits's'(2,40;2,51). The 'kowping' calls (2,47;2,49) are generally higher-pitched than the Moorhen and often have a squealing, trilled tone, reminiscent of a Water Rail, but quite variable. Frequently goes in a skimming, half-walking flight over the water, producing a rhythmic splashing.

# OYSTERCATCHERS - HAEMATOPODIDAE

**Oystercatcher**   *Haematopus ostralegus*                    2,64;2,72;2,85
Oystercatchers are very vocal birds with fairly loud piping voices. In flight they frequently call a 't-peep'(2,72); when alarmed and scolding an intruder this becomes a piercing 'peep-peep-peep'. Display occurs between males in status disputes and between a pair in courtship; it can be heard at any time of the year and consists of lengthy passages of bubbling piping and trills building out of the more usual calls (2,85).

This can be heard from a couple or frequently from a group of several birds; often accompanied by ritual posturing with the head lowered and bill pointing down or with wings raised above the back. On their breeding grounds from March, display or nuptial chases are frequent, with several birds calling repeatedly and stridently (2,64)

## AVOCETS - RECURVIROSTRIDAE

**Avocet**   *Recurvirostra avosetta*
Generally moving in flocks and breeding in colonies, the Avocet can be quite a vociferous bird, but with a very limited vocal range. Usually calls a repeated, short 'kleep' or 'klew' in a piping voice; this tends to become more strident and rapid from an alarmed bird. Displaying birds give a softer, piping twitter in the same voice.

## STONE-CURLEWS - BURHINIDAE

**Stone-curlew**   *Burhinus oedicnemus*                                1,45
The Stone Curlew is another species better known in the past in many areas for its voice. Birds are heard to call during the day, but at night they become much more vocal in display. Their most characteristic call is a drawn-out, piping 'wail', often a variation on a 'cour-lee' motif, hence the 'curlew' in its name, though only distantly related to the Curlew. In display this may be accompanied by some churring, Partridge-like notes. Also gives a call with a single long note in a similar voice to the 'cour-lee'. Birds tend to call a short, repeated, churring or piping note in alarm. The wailing cries can usually be heard a mile away on a calm night. Birds are on their northern breeding grounds between April and August.

## PLOVERS - CHARADRIIDAE

**Little Ringed Plover**   *Charadrius dubius*
Can be quite a vocal bird, general calls include variations on a piping 'tree-oo' or 'tyew', thin and high-pitched, in a slightly trilling voice or sometimes with a purer timbre. Calls of this type become more rapid and strident from an anxious bird. In display and courtship, calling becomes more rhythmic, and incorporates clucks, trillings and whistles, broadly similar to the Ringed Plover.

**Ringed Plover**   *Charadrius hiaticula*                                2,73
Quiet for long periods, the Ringed Plover is probably heard most

frequently calling a curlew-like, but higher-pitched and thinner 'tu-wee', which may become a single, rising note 'wheep', more strident from an anxious bird. But as Spring progresses and display and courtship intensify, birds become much more vocal with a variety of song motifs (2,73). Often beginning with repeated 'wheep-wheep' calls, builds into rhythmic repetitions of cluckings, churrings and more melodic 't-lee-u's, often given in a short, ritualised song-flight. Peak of vocal activity is probably April and May.

### Kentish Plover   *Charadrius alexandrinus*
Calls with a wide variety of soft trilling motifs, usually repeated in runs; sometimes includes some louder, more piping 'wheep's, but even these have a slight trill to them.

### Dotterel   *Charadrius morinellus*
On the high tops, so often silent apart from the sighing of the wind, listen out for a faint, plaintive 'peep': somewhere near, remarkably well camouflaged for such a colouful bird, is a Dotterel concerned at your presence. Heard from close-by, or from a more anxious bird, the 'peep' may become more substantial. Birds also give trilling and piping calls with a variety of motifs in display, both on the ground and in swift aerial chases. Sometimes these may be so thin as to have a tinkling sound to them. Birds taking flight frequently give a trilled, piping call.

### Golden Plover   *Pluvialis apricaria*                                    2,14;2,18
The most frequently encountered call of the Golden Plover on their breeding grounds is a plaintive-sounding, pure 'too', usually given when an intruder enters their breeding area, but birds seem to use it for contact too (2,14). Birds on territory also call to each other with a 'du-lu-deeoo' in a similar voice, or simply a descending 'deeoo' (2,18), which is possibly another form of song. Displaying males sing a repeated three-note pattern (two high pitched, leading a lower-pitched rising slur) in a voice with a hint of a trill, often in display flight (2,14). Winter flocks begin breaking up and moving towards their upland breeding areas around the end of March and begin flocking again in lowland fields from August. Flocking calls include a variety of motifs with a hint of the song.

### Grey Plover   *Pluvialis squatarola*
Wintering birds and birds on passage are occasionally heard calling a distinctive, melodic whistle 'tlu-ee', the 'tlu' descending sharply in pitch and the 'ee' rising.

**Lapwing**   *Vanellus vanellus*                                         2,1
Fairly vocal birds at any time of the year, Lapwings frequently call on
their breeding grounds with various 'peew's, often with a distinct wheezing timbre, which become more rapid, emphatic and strident when a
bird is alarmed. In their wild, aerial displays birds sing rhythmic, whooping versions of their call, often accompanied by purring wheezes, interspersed with headlong dives towards the ground and slow ritualised
wing-beats. Display begins on fine days in the late Winter before the
wintering flocks break up and move inland, as birds occasionally take to
the air and display above the flock; at such times the flock can become a
babble of calls.

## SANDPIPERS & ALLIES - SCOLOPACIDAE

**Knot**   *Calidris canutus*
Generally quite a quiet bird, Knots call with quite a strident 'weep,
weep' or a low 'knut' (hence the name). On their breeding grounds
displaying birds call with a variety of simple, fluting, whistled motifs.
Winter flocks can become vociferous to the point of producing a wall of
noise.

**Sanderling**   *Calidris alba*
Sanderlings call occasionally with various, short, squeaking 'whit's or
'wick's. In display, calling becomes more varied and rapidly delivered.
Flocks can get quite vociferous and become a mass of chattering

**Little Stint**   *Calidris minuta*
Little Stints generally call with repeated, abrupt 'chit's, usually heard as
a soft chittering. In display this builds to runs of repeated, squeaky,
sibilant notes 'tsee-tsee-tsee...'.

**Temminck's Stint**   *Calidris temminckii*
Displaying males sing from the air with a squeaking 'tsee-tsee-tsee...',
similar to, but fuller than, the Little Stint. This builds through various
tempo changes to a rapid, sibilant trilling. Birds can be heard on their
breeding grounds from mid May to late June.

**Purple Sandpiper**   *Calidris maritima*
Calls occasionally, but softly in Winter; becomes more vocal on its
breeding grounds. Calls include Little Grebe-like, laughing trills; rising,
slightly trilled whistles, like a Dunlin, but of a purer tone; an abrupt
'wit-wit' call, and motifs built out of variations of this call.

## Dunlin   *Calidris alpina*                                         2,13;2,73

In winter flocks, Dunlin frequently call to each other softly, but this is not usually heard at any distance. As breeding approaches in the Spring, display becomes more frequent and prolonged and birds become more vocal. In their breeding areas from around April, birds are often very vocal. Males sing in flight above their nesting territories and birds sing and call frequently around their feeding pools. Their voice is a distinctive rapidly-trilled whistle. General calls include single trilled whistles and variable short motifs in this voice; in song these become more formal, lengthened into a repeated trilling, rising quickly to a shrill intensity, then gradually subsiding (2,13). Also frequently calls with repeated, rising trills in a lower-pitched, 'nasal' voice, suggestive of a frog croaking (2,73 with Ringed Plover;2,15 with Red-throated Diver). Birds also have a variety of very abrupt, single note calls.

## Ruff   *Philomachus pugnax*

Ruff are rarely heard and generally seem to be a silent bird. Males have a lekking courtship system, but display seems to be wholly visual. Alarmed birds may call a short, double-note croak, sometimes trisyllabic.

## Jack Snipe   *Lymnocryptes minimus*

Not particularly vocal birds, Jack Snipe occasionally call with a churring croak. In their breeding areas males display in flight with a variety of strange sounds repeated in almost mechanical rhythms, some vocal, some produced by drumming like Snipe; these range from bubbling or whooping sounds to tinkling chatter, like a row of dominoes falling.

## Snipe   *Gallinago gallinago*                                       2,36;2,57

For much of the year silent birds, Snipe usually call if flushed, with a repeated, screechy 'skrrrp' as they zip away on fast wing-beats often on a zig-zag path. On their breeding grounds Snipe become much more vocal. Birds sing a repetitive, 'yikker', 'chipper' or 'ticker' song (different names for the same vocal) - repeated double or single notes in a throaty or squeaky voice (2,36); This may be given from the ground, from a fence post or in low flight. Birds also display high in the air in an undulating flight; on the descents the birds beat their wings hard and spread their tails like a fan to produce a throbbing, bleating sound known as 'drumming' (2,57). Drumming (and the yikkering song) can be heard at any time of the day or night, but is probably most frequent in the early morning and evening, and in brighter intervals between showers on a wet day through Spring into Summer.

**Woodcock** *Scolopax rusticola* 1,54

Generally a very silent bird during the Autumn and Winter, immigrant Woodcocks have been said to give soft whistling calls on arriving at the coast. Flushed birds occasionally give a soft, sharp grunt, but usually only the rapid wing-beats are heard and the bird has disappeared through the trees. In their breeding areas, from fine nights around February, birds begin their 'roding' displays. Males fly around their territorial boundaries with slow-motion wing-beats, calling repeatedly a croaking 'orr-orr-irt' followed by a sharp squeak (1,54). The squeak can often be heard at several hundred yards, but you need to be a little closer to hear the croak. Occasionally a dispute occurs and a chase ensues with repeated excited squeaking. Roding takes place at dawn and dusk. If you come across a roding Woodcock it is worth waiting at the spot for 10 minutes; there is a good chance the bird will come round the same circuit again in a little while.

**Black-tailed Godwit** *Limosa limosa*

The Black-tailed Godwit can be a fairly vocal bird, particularly in the breeding season. Birds call with a variety of motifs and single notes, usually in a thin, Lapwing like voice, but including quite shrill chitterings, Buzzard-like mews and some partridge-like scratchy notes. In display birds sing various motifs in regular repetition, such as 'teu-wu-pawu, teu-wupawu...' or a Snipe-like 'wicka-wicka-wicka...'.

**Bar-tailed Godwit** *Limosa lapponica*

Generally silent during the Winter months, occasionally a bird will make a zig-zag display flight over the water, calling single or repeated shrill 'kek's or sometimes a snatch of song 'kawuk-kawuk-kawuk...'. But generally Bar-tailed Godwits only become vocal with display in their breeding areas.

**Whimbrel** *Numenius phaeopus* 2,75

Often calls in flight with a repeated, piping note, almost a trill, lasting a second or more, in a Curlew-like voice, but high-pitched and thinner (2,75). The male's song in display, usually only heard in their breeding areas, is very similar in form to the Curlew, but not usually so long or elaborate, and with the bubbling sounding more of a slightly shrill trill, as in the flight call. Birds also call with long plaintive whistles like the Curlew, but again in a thinner voice.

**Curlew** *Numenius arquata* 2,2;2,77

A vocal bird throughout the year, in Autumn and Winter Curlews tend to call with variations around 'coor-coor' or 'klee-klee' and the eponymous 'curlee', all usually repeated several times (2,77). As Spring advances and birds begin to move towards their breeding areas, song and other display calls are heard more frequently. In display males rise into the air, often almost vertically, with soft 'coor' type calls building gradually into long bubbling trills (2,2). Birds in the air above their territories call in long, plaintive whistles for quite lengthy periods, often with birds on adjacent territories calling at the same time in the distance. Song is frequent in the morning and evening, occasional at night and quite frequent during the day, especially in finer breaks in stormy weather or with an approaching storm. Display seems to pass over a moor like a wave: one or two birds start up and soon the whole community is in voice, then after a while all goes quiet again. Birds often call with the 'coor-coor' and 'curlee' motifs when an intruder enters the area; when birds become more anxious, they break into a harsh 'cucucucucu'.

**Spotted Redshank**   *Tringa erythropus*
In their Wintering grounds, most often heard to call an abrupt, whistling 'chew-wee'; also has a repeated 'chip' call in a lower voice like the other shanks, which in display may break into trills. Song, heard in the breeding areas, is an elongated fluting 'tchew-wee-oo' repeated.

**Redshank**   *Tringa totanus*                                    2,20;2,78;2,87
Vocal throughout the year, Redshanks often call with a lengthy, piped 'teu', 'teu-hu-hu' or similar motif as they move about on their feeding grounds (2,78;2,87). Birds in a roosting flock often make soft, squeaking calls; also has a repeated 'chip' call and other whistles. Calling becomes more rapid when a bird is excited, and more shrill when anxious. Song, which can be heard from early Spring through to the Summer, is a fluted 'tu-lee-oo' repeated several times, usually in a short flight (2,20).

**Greenshank**   *Tringa nebularia*                                        2,16
Although in many ways quite a solitary bird, the Greenshank is surprisingly vocal, certainly so in the breeding season, with a wide repertoire of calls and variations of song. At anytime of the year calls with a Redshank-like 'teu-teu-teu', but thinner and often at a quicker tempo, and a repeated 'chip' call like the Redshank; more distinct are a full 'chu-chu-chu', frequently given when flushed, and various fluted motifs. Song is heard as the birds arrive in their breeding areas from around early April through to early Summer. It consists in sometimes long passages of a repeated, fluted, double-note motif, such as 'klu-hi, klu-hi, klu-hi...' or

similar. Males sing in flight, sometimes at a great height above their territories and also when they come in to the water's edge to feed and leave again.

**Green Sandpiper**   *Tringa ochropus*
Often calls with a sweet, thin, piping call 'tluee-tli-tli-tli'; and when alarmed with a sharp, repeated 'chip, chip'. In display flight birds sing repeated, liquid, piping motifs, similar to the first call mentioned.

**Wood Sandpiper**   *Tringa glareola*
Calls with a repeated, abrupt 'wee-wee' in flight and a 'chew-hew'; more anxious birds call a shrill 'chip' or 'chit', often repeated rapidly into a chattering trill. In song-flight birds repeat a whistling 'teu-lu' motif or similar.

**Common Sandpiper**   *Actitis hypoleucos*                       2,62;2,64
Common Sandpipers are generally very vocal in their breeding areas. Their voice is a high-pitched, thin pipe and frequently heard is a fairly quick 'teu-hu-hu-hu', descending in pitch. With an intruder near, birds call an elongated 'tee' (in the background on 2,61) or a slow 'tee-hee-hee'. The song given from the ground and in flight is a repeated, sharp tinkling 'titiwee-tihi' or similar (2,62;2,64). Song is heard from when the birds arrive in April through to the Summer, but becomes less frequent.

**Turnstone**   *Arenaria interpres*
Although rarely heard, Turnstones give occasional low calls in their Winter feeding areas, stuttering tu-tuk's and 'tchew-hu's. In display on their breeding grounds, birds sing with squeaky chatterings, often becoming rattling trills. Birds call a fast, squeaky, low 'titi-weeky-weehihi' or such-like, when alarmed.

**Red-necked Phalarope**   *Phalaropus lobatus*
Birds in a flock communicate with fast chittering calls. Sometimes the 'chit's are given more emphatically as single notes. In display birds sing with similar chittering to the flocking calls, often with some longer, Dunlin-like, wheezing notes.

# SKUAS - STERCORARIIDAE

**Arctic Skua**   *Stercorarius parasiticus*
Not heard very often, birds have a low 'chut-uk' call and various 'chak's and short, croaky mews. Displaying birds give a repeated, rising, mewing yodel.

**Long-tailed Skua**   *Stercorarius longicaudus*
Generally quiet except in their breeding areas, birds call with a thin
'kree', particularly when alarmed. This can vary to a Buzzard-like mew.
Other calls, also used in display fall somewhere between the squeal of a
Common Gull and the mewing of a Buzzard.

**Great Skua**   *Stercorarius skua*
Generally quiet, Great Skuas give brief, croaking 'chuck's and 'ug's,
when an intruder approaches the nest site, and follow up with dive-
bombing attacks, sometimes with rasping calls.

## GULLS - LARIDAE

Most of the gull species have a more or less similar vocabulary and, in
distinguishing between the species, pitch and tone of voice become
more important indicators. The different species all give variations of
short gruff calls and longer, squealing calls. Most species have a long
call, with a more formal structure, which acts like a song. Display calls
can be heard at virtually any time of year, outside the breeding season
serving as status claims.

**Mediterranean Gull**   *Larus melanocephalus*
Birds give a light 'caw' or 'kaa' call, with something of a yelp and a
'nasal' tone to it. Very similar in voice to its close relative the Black-
headed Gull.

**Little Gull**   *Larus minutus*
Little Gulls have a thin, quite raspy voice; calling is based on trailing
'kaa's and sharper 'kek's, repeated in varying rhythmic patterns, often
merging into a chattering rattle.

**Black-headed Gull**   *Larus ridibundus*                    1,5;2,88
The Black-headed Gull is a very vocal bird, with a multitude of variations on a basic hoarse, slightly grating 'kaaar' call. It becomes sharp,
and often a staccato bark or repeated yelp, when a bird is alarmed; a
repeated yelp, in disputes; and becomes so variable in display, that it is
difficult to describe, but the delivery tends to be more rhythmic and
build to crescendos of excitement (2,88). Breeding colonies can be very
noisy, especially when birds are settling after a disturbance.

**Common Gull**   *Larus canus*                              2,63
Common Gulls frequently call sharp, thin 'kow's in flight and short,
mewed squeals, which becomes more strident when alarmed. In status

and courtship displays birds call with longer squeals 'kee-you', descending in pitch, often in accelerated repetition to crescendos of excitement, then settling into softer elongated 'kow's. The full display call has a mixture of several long squeals and passages of repeated, emphatic 'ka-ka-ka..'s'.

**Lesser Black-backed Gull**  *Larus fuscus*  2,71
Probably not quite so vocal as the Herring Gull, Lesser Black-backs have a similar set of calls, but their voice has more of a croaking, throaty timbre. Frequently calls a repeated 'ow-ow-ow' with much fuller notes than the yapping call of a Herring Gull, but not as deep-voiced as a Great Black-back; also calls with single 'kow's' (2,71), often sustained to the point of becoming a hoarse, broken squeals. The full display call is similar in form to the Herring Gull, but rarely given at such volume, and with a thinner, rougher voice, often accompanied by mewing moans.

**Herring Gull**  *Larus argentatus*  2,67;2,72
Frequently vocal, the Herring gull's calls, like most of the other Gulls, are made up of yelping squeals or mews 'kay-ou' and shorter 'kow's, both variable in delivery (2,72). The squeals generally have more depth to them than the similar calls of the Common Gull, and often have a break in the pitch like a yodel. Both calls are used in alarm at an intruder, and frequently the 'kow's are run together in a yapping 'ka-ka-ka-ka-ka', not at full voice. The full display call or song builds from several powerful squeals into a loud, 'laughing' 'yah-yah-yah...', which carries far (2,67), frequently heard in sea-side towns and harbours. Large flocks often give off a groaning rumble, as birds voice low, gutteral moans to each other.

**Great Black-backed Gull**  *Larus marinus*  2,66;2,70
Most frequently heard from the Great Black-back is the 'kaow' call, similar to the Herring and Lesser Black-back, but in a deep, throaty, strangled voice; often accompanied by 'ow-ow-ow-ow's in a similar throaty voice, especially when given in alarm at an intruder (2,70). The full display call is a repeated, laughing 'aow-aow-aow...', given as powerful, throaty half-squeals (2,66).

**Kittiwake**  *Rissa tridactyla*  2,91
Kittiwake breeding colonies can be very noisy indeed, as greeting displays between a pair, set off adjacent pairs and frequently it seems the whole colony is calling at full voice with their piercing calls. Their most distinctive form of call is usually rendered the eponymous 'kitti-wayke'

with the last syllable often drawn out, usually repeated in a series. Birds frequently call with single, abrupt, cawing 'ka's. Displaying birds quickly build to louder 'kitti-wayke's, quietening only gradually through various moanings and groanings.

# TERNS - STERNIDAE

The terns are generally very vocal birds - certainly all the sociable terns (which covers our more common species). They have a distinctive grating sound to their voices, but the different species are not always easy to separate by voice alone. They are especially vocal around their nesting colonies. When calling in alarm or scolding an intruder near the nesting area, their voices are particularly harsh. In greeting and court-ship displays, their voices are not quite so hard-edged, and the calls do carry some formal elaboration. Display does take place on the ground, but perhaps more frequently in the air around the breeding colony, especially when one of a pair returns with food.

**Sandwich Tern**　*Sterna sandvicensis*　　　　　　　　　　2,68
The most distinctive call of the Sandwich Tern is an emphatically disyllabic 'kay-rrick', sometimes a more hurried 'kirrick', rising to a higher pitch on the second syllable; given in various circumstances, including display. Also has a thin, high pitched 'kir-kir-kir...', which may introduce the 'kay-rrick', and sharp 'kek's. Alarmed birds at a nesting colony give a low, staccato cackling.

**Roseate Tern**　*Sterna dougallii*
Roseate Terns often call with various harsh, monosyllabic 'krrr's, rang-ing from high and slightly squeaky to lower-pitched and growling; more distinctive is a rapid, scratchy 'chee-vee' or similar. In display flight, calling becomes more rhythmic and elaborate, often incorporating short, soft, high-pitched squeals.

**Common Tern**　*Sterna hirundo*　　　　　　　　　　　　2,69
Most distinctive of the calls of the Common Tern are a hurried, repeti-tive 'kierri-kierri-kierri...' and a harsh, sustained 'kee-aarrr' with the emphasis more to the second syllable. Also frequently calls an abrupt, squeaking 'jiff' similar to the Arctic and rattled chatterings in alarm.

**Arctic Tern**　*Sterna paradisaea*　　　　　　　　　　　2,74
The Arctic Tern frequently calls a 'kee-err' with emphasis on the 'kee' and often a squealing tone to it; a rapid-fire, repeated 'ke-ke-ke-keerr', varying in tone from lower and rasping to higher and squealing, is

common in display and fairly distinctive. Like the Common, frequently calls a sharp 'jiff' and scolds an intruder with a machine gun-like, repeated, sharp rasp.

**Little Tern**   *Sterna albifrons*
The Little Tern's voice is less rasping than the previous terns; in display tends to call with a rhythmically erratic, churring chatter, reminiscent in form to the twitterings of a Swallow. Also has a 'jiff' call like the Common and Arctic, but is not so sharp, with a softer 'j'.

**Black Tern**   *Chlidonias niger*
Not often heard, the Black Tern's most usual calls are a thinnish 'kurr-da' or similar, often repeated and with the emphasis on the first syllable, and a short 'krik', possibly the equivalent of the 'jiff' calls in the other terns.

## AUKS - ALCIDAE

The auks become fairly vocal around their breeding colonies; certainly this is where we usually hear them. Birds call in display and in disputes between neighbours. In the closer nesting species, like the Guillemot, calling between one or two birds often sets the neighbours off.

**Guillemot**   *Uria aalge*                                      2,92
Usual calls are a long, drawn-out 'aaarr' and shorter repeated 'arr-arr-arr...'. Guillemots have more of a 'squawk' to their voice than Razorbills and, especially when heard at a distance, calling may have a 'cooing' quality.

**Razorbill**   *Alca torda*                                      2,93
Razorbills have formally similar calls to Guillemots, but in a deeper, more growling voice. The long 'aawrr' has a distinct rolling 'r' to it, and, when the call slows or subsides, can sound ratchety. Pairs tend not to nest in close proximity, so individual calls are usually more distinct than the Guillemot.

**Black Guillemot**   *Cepphus grylle*
The Black Guillemot's display calls are distinctive, and markedly different from the other auks. Their voice is a high-pitched, thin whistle, often described as bell-like; calling is in the form of longer whistles that descend slightly in pitch, giving a plaintive quality, and in rapidly-alternated, two note motifs.

### Little Auk   *Alle alle*
Calls are quite variable and include repeated whoops, yelps, tittering laughs and Guillemot-like 'aarr's, but in a higher and thinner voice.

### Puffin   *Fratercula arctica*
Calls are of a similar form to the Guillemot and Razorbill, but in a moaning or groaning voice, sounding more like a rolling 'aaah', with subsiding repetitions. Pitch is varied to give a 'sing-song' quality. Mostly heard resonating from their nesting burrows.

## PIGEONS - COLUMBIDAE

The pigeon family are well known for their purring and crooning voices, usually heard from singing males performing little dances with their breasts swollen with air or perched high in a woodland canopy. This family are also prone to making display-flights, often including wing-clapping sounds.

### Rock Dove/Feral Pigeon   *Columba livia*                    1,9
Display calls include various throaty purring notes; a more recognisable kind of song-motif is the frequently heard cooing to the rhythm of 'bucket-a-coo' repeated over.

### Stock Dove   *Columba oenas*                    1,70
The Stock Dove sings with resonant disyllabic cooing, a repeated 'cooo-uh' with the second syllable usually dropping in pitch. They come repeated briskly in runs of around six at intervals; calls within a run tend to build slightly in tempo and pitch. Birds generally sing from a high branch just under the woodland canopy or a rock ledge and can be heard at any time of the year, but mainly between February and July.

### Woodpigeon   *Columba palumbus*                    1,13
The song of the Wood Pigeon is a frequently-heard sound in woodland and anywhere where a few trees or bushes provide some security. The usual form of the song is a deep, cooing 'cu-coo-coo, cu-coo', with the second syllable emphasised and of a higher pitch; it can sound pure in tone, but is often husky when heard close to (1,13 and throughout the sequence). Birds frequently sing from quite low perches in the middle of thick bushes, as well as the woodland canopy. Also heard are quieter repeated cooing groans. Birds frequently display in open woodland and over the canopy in an undulating flight: birds clap their wings as they rise in the air, then glide a short way losing height before repeating the cycle.

**Collared Dove**   *Streptopelia decaocto*                                    1,17
An increasingly common bird in our area over the last few decades, the
Collared Dove has become the optimist's Cuckoo. The usual form of
the song is a resonant 'coo-coo-coo', the middle syllable emphasised and
the last syllable abrupt, usually with a pure tone of voice, and at a higher
pitch than the other doves and pigeons; but variations are heard. Frequently calls in flight (usually coming in to land) with a dry, wheezing
'whew' and displays with wing-claps.

**Turtle Dove**   *Streptopelia turtur*                                        2,29
The Turtle Dove sings in lengthy passages of a rippling purr, usually to
a repeated rhythm of 'courr-cor-cor'. Heard from close-by, each rendition is accompanied by a quiet wheezing gulp. When first heard, the
sound might appear more appropriate to the croaking of an amphibian,
than a bird.

# PARROTS - PSITTACIDAE

**Ring-necked Parakeet**   *Psittacula krameri*
The most frequently-heard call, is a repeated, shrill 'kee-kee-kee...',
often given in flight, and reminiscent of a kestrel or other small hawk.

# CUCKOOS - CUCULIDAE

**Cuckoo**   *Cuculus canorus*                                                 1,80
Few people can be unaware of the territorial song of the male Cuckoo -
a repeated, far-carrying, pure 'cu-ckoo'. But individual birds produce
variations on the theme, often adding a third 'coo'. Listen out for the
Collared Dove: people occasionally confuse the songs of the two species. The song can be heard from when the birds return to their breeding
range from around mid-April and traditionally symbolises the arrival of
Spring. They are said to change their tune in June: when the peak of
sexual activity has passed, it is as if their voices break and their eponymous call becomes weaker and croaky. Song dies out in July. Males also
produce cackling (and spitting) calls in status disputes. A fairly loud,
bubbling trill is frequently heard from females, similar to, but fuller and
less shrill than a Little Grebe's whinnying.

# BARN OWLS - TYTONIDAE

**Barn Owl**   *Tyto alba*                                                     1,31
The 'Screech Owl' of old: the male's territorial call is a strident screech,

only given occasionally. Birds also call with less strident, similar raspy or snoring calls, especially round the nest site. Young birds threaten an unwelcome visitor with rasping hisses.

## OWLS - STRIGIDAE

**Snowy Owl**   *Nyctea scandiaca*
Generally quiet away from the breeding site; calls include short, gutteral croaks, deep, husky 'hoo's and hawk-like yelps and whistles.

**Little Owl**   *Athene noctua*                                                    1,47
Often vociferous birds, including during the day, the male's song is a medium-length, tonally quite pure, loud 'whoo-ee' with a yodelling rise in pitch on the 'ee' (1,47). In other situations birds call with a variety of loud squealing yelps; these become more staccato and grating, some-times including a piercing 'kek-kek-kek..' when a bird is alarmed.

**Tawny Owl**   *Strix aluco*                                                       1,58
Tawnies are probably the most frequently heard of the North European owls and are the source of the classic 'to-whit-to-whoo', (though I have never actually heard a call resembling this phrase myself); both males and females call frequently, at most times of the year, particularly at dusk and dawn. The male's hoot is quite variable, ranging from long pure hoots, sometimes with a huskiness, a tremulousness or a slight shriek when a bird is excited, to a variety of melodic motifs, with distinct syllables, approaching the legendary rendition cited above. The female calls a sharp 'kewick'. Young birds produce more variations, though often in a thinner slightly higher voice.

**Long-eared Owl**   *Asio otus*
Generally quite a silent owl and mostly nocturnal, the Long-eared becomes more vocal in the breeding season. The male sings a deep, quite short, repeated 'hoo'; the female has a similar song, but with a wheezing timbre. Neither hoots carry far. Display often includes wing-clapping. Birds also call with abrupt, low, wheezing barks. Young birds produce various squeals and mews.

**Short-eared Owl**   *Asio flammeus*
Generally a quiet bird, the Short-eared Owl can be quite vocal in the breeding season and occasionally during the winter months. The male's song is a steady series of short, deep hoots 'hoo-hoo-hoo...'. Display may include wing-clapping. Birds also call with various, wheezing yelps

and barks, sometimes softer like a purring exhalation of breath (later in 1,40). Calls and song are often heard during the day, but early and late.

## NIGHTJARS - CAPRIMULGIDAE

**Nightjar**   *Caprimulgus europaeus*                                    1,48
The 'churring' song of the male Nightjar must be one of the most evocative and hypnotic sounds of the twilight hours; something like a steady rattling trill, rising and falling in pitch at rhythmic intervals. Birds sustain this 'drone' for quite long passages, often ending with an odd series of churrs like a machine slowing down. Birds usually sing from a horizontal branch, occasionally from the ground or in flight; most frequently heard at dawn and dusk, often during the night and very occasionally during the day. Females have been heard to produce a similar sound from the nest. The Nightjar's churring is fairly distinctive, but similar to the stridulation of the Mole Cricket. Birds sometimes produce wing-clapping in display. Song can be heard from when the birds arrive in May through to early August and occasionally in September before they leave. Birds also frequently give a slightly nasal 'kwick' call, with a sharp rise in pitch and a wheezing 'kuhu'.

## SWIFTS - APODIDAE

**Swift**   *Apus apus*                                               1,12
The swift is only with us for some 3 months, between May and August; but for many of us their wild aerial parties will always be associated with the balmy evenings of high summer. In the evening the birds of an area gather in groups and indulge in high-speed flying chases, often joining in a chorus of 'screaming', reaching a peak of activity at dusk; and then all goes quiet and the birds have disappeared. The screaming, when heard close by, is actually a fast, high-pitched trill.

## KINGFISHERS - ALCEDINIDAE

**Kingfisher**   *Alcedo atthis*                                  2,56;2,58
Frequently calls in flight, a fairly loud, clear whistle, reminiscent of a Dunnock's call but more strident and descending slightly in pitch. Alarmed birds call more intensely. General contact calls tend to be softer, slight-trilled whistles, repeated with some elaboration in display.

## HOOPOES - UPUPIDAE

**Hoopoe**   *Upupa epops*
The male's song, from which the bird gets its name, is a repeated, abrupt 'hoo-hoo-hoo' - usually three given in series and quite far-carrying. Alarmed birds give a harsh, breathy squawk.

## WOODPECKERS - PICIDAE

**Wryneck**   *Jynx torquilla*
The male's song is a penetrating 'kee-kee-kee...', with a hint of a squeaky toy in its tone; also often rendered 'kew-kew-kew...' and described as 'laughing'. The female gives a similar song, but in a more hoarse, raspy voice. Reported to drum occasionally.

**Green Woodpecker**   *Picus viridis*                                          1,75
The Green Woodpecker is only heard to drum very occasionally. It is much better known from its 'yaffling' call, which sounds something like a shrill laugh. This serves as a territorial call, an alarm call and probably for general contact, with appropriate variations in intensity and repetition, and can be heard throughout the year. Individuals are said to produce a soft 'twee-twee-twee' occasionally in courtship.

**Great Spotted Woodpecker**   *Dendrocopos major*                              1,59
Drums frequently in spring, though it is heard occasionally at other times of the year. The Great-spotted also frequently calls a loud, abrupt 'pip' or 'chek', which becomes more strident and rapidly repeated as a bird becomes alarmed and occasionally run together in a rattling trill. Can also be heard tapping on wood more softly.

**Lesser Spotted Woodpecker**   *Dendrocopos minor*                             1,60
A small bird that usually stays in the tree tops, the Lesser Spotted Woodpecker is easily missed without hearing its call or drumming. It drums quite frequently, not always producing a thinner sound than the Great Spotted; its drumming is in slightly longer, more even bursts than that of the Great Spotted, which fades slightly at the end. Also calls a shrill, rapid 'pee-pee-pee...', like a Kestrel.

## LARKS - ALAUDIDAE

**Woodlark**   *Lullula arborea*                                                1,46
Woodlarks can be heard singing at almost any time of the year, but most frequently between February and July. Song is in lengthy passages of

repeated fluting notes at a leisurely rhythm; each run lasting between about four and eight seconds, usually falling in pitch and slowing towards the end slightly in tempo. Usually includes variations on 'lu-lu-lu...' phrases (hence its generic name). Song is produced perched and in flight, and is sometimes heard at night. In song-flight birds don't hover like a Skylark, but tend to make a wide fluttering circle back to near their starting point. Calls are like song notes: 'too-lu-ee' and 'wee-ou' are often heard.

**Skylark**   *Alauda arvensis*                                    1,30;2,82
So often before dawn and just before the first Robins and Blackbirds start to sing in the surrounding woods, the first Skylark is heard from the open fields. Sometimes birds sing while perched, but usually a bird takes off and begins singing, while gradually rising vertically on fluttering wings to become a speck in the sky. The song is liquid and 'chirping', continuing unbroken for long periods - sometimes 10 or 15 minutes, frequently containing mimicry of other species (1,30 and can be heared in the Flow Country sequence). Skylarks like the sun for singing; on mixed days in the early Spring, as the sun comes out for a while, so they rise into the air singing, though it may be blowing near a gale. Song can be heard occasionally at any time of the year, but most frequently from late Winter through to Summer. Heard calling quite frequently at any time of the year with various 'chirrup' motifs (2,82).

**Shore Lark**   *Eremophila alpestris*
Most frequent call is a pipit-like, tremulous 'tseep'; also has a call made up of a run of softly-whistled notes, rising in pitch, like a half-song. Song, often given in flight, is like the Skylark, but more hesitant and lacking the power and exuberance.

## SWALLOWS AND MARTINS - HIRUNDINIDAE

Although the martin species tend to breed colonially, but the Swallow in more isolated pairs, all three species here are very sociable and vocal. Birds call frequently in flight with constant variation on their basic calls and voice, often giving the impression of vigorous chatter; song, though rambling rather than stereotyped, tends to be a more formal elaboration of calling themes in a similar voice, with a few recurring motifs. In pre-migration flocking, parties of birds become very vocal, though not usually in full voice, where the calling becomes a kind of communal subsong, mainly heard in the morning and evening around the roost.

**Sand Martin**  *Riparia riparia*                                                2,55

In general flock activity, foraging and around the nesting colony, Sand Martins call with a warbling chatter in a slightly buzzy, churring or trilled voice. Difficult to distinguish particular calls in the general chatter, but a wheezing 'chee', descending in pitch, is commonly heard. As a rule, sequences of notes tend to be varied little in pitch and tone, and more in the rhythm of their delivery (cf House Martin). Quite a vocal bird during the breeding season in the north.

**Swallow**  *Hirundo rustica*                                              1,22;1,23

Swallows call and sing throughout their breeding season in the North, at any time of the day from first light to late in the evening. Song is a liquid, twittering sequence of slightly squeaky notes and clicking trills, produced in lengthy passages with short, hesitant pauses (1,23 after the Mistle Thrush calls). Sometimes produced in snatches on the wing, but frequently in long sessions from a perch. Swallows also call frequently on the wing with a terse 'vit, chee-vit', each syllable rising in pitch, and a 'chi-zee' or 'chissik' (cf Pied Wagtail 'chissik') and other motifs, often interspersed with snatches of song (1,22).

**House Martin**  *Delichon urbica*                                           1,29

House Martins tend to call frequently on the wing in the vicinity of their breeding colony, possibly less so when a flock is foraging further afield. Their voice is similar to the Sand Martin, but less rattling, with more of a bubbling trill and with more melodic and tonal variation than the Sand Martin. General calls often figure a clipped, trilled 'chu-chu' repeated with a multitude of slight variation, sometimes given in longish broken runs. Song is sometimes given in snatches on the wing, but usually in the vicinity of the nest and more often actually in, or perched beside the nest; song is a surprisingly musical, soft twittering, incorporating short, bubbling trills, and delivered at a hurried tempo. Anxious birds call with a repeated 'tcheu', descending in pitch.

## PIPITS AND WAGTAILS - MOTACILLIDAE

The pipits are fairly vocal birds, often calling unobtrusively in contact while going about their business, calling readily in alarm, and singing frequently. Fullest song is given in flight, often beginning with a building repeated note as the bird rises, breaking into a varied series of trills and wheezes as the bird descends on parachuting wings. These three species have broadly similar vocabularies and singing styles and can be difficult to separate on voice without practice - certainly the call notes. Habitat is a useful starting point. The wagtails have broadly similar sounding voices and calls to the pipits, but their calls are subject to much variation and birds often seem to sing with fairly regular repetitions of one or more call notes. Occasionally the males of these three species deliver sustained passages of more intense, 'twittering' song; this is not often heard and is easily overlooked, as it is not usually given in full voice. Pipits and wagtails call readily in flight, the wagtail species with easily recognised calls.

**Tree Pipit**  *Anthus trivialis*                                      1,53

Each song of the Tree Pipit, whether perched or rising into a song-flight (usually from a tree - cf Meadow Pipit), often begins with a series of Chaffinch-like 'teu-teu-teu-teu...'s; when singing from a perch, that may be it, or it may lead into several further distinct phrases, but it still remains a 'half-song' compared to the full song in flight. A bird may sing a dozen perched songs before launching into the air, or just a few; the full song is made up of distinct phrases, like the perched song, but is much extended, incorporating other chaffinch-like repeated notes, wag-tail-like phrases, fast clicking trills and most distinctively a slowing series of longer 'whee-whee-whee...' notes, rising in pitch. Song can be heard in the breeding areas from April to July, at any time of day in fine weather, but most frequently in the early morning and early evening. The flight call is a wheezing 'tsee, tsee' and more anxious birds call a wheezy 'dwee, dwee', rising in pitch, and a clearer, abrupt, ringing 'tee, tee'. A fairly vocal bird, the Tree Pipit's full song is something of a gem, redolent of the sun shining on some open-wooded hillside or heath in summer.

**Meadow Pipit**  *Anthus pratensis*                                2,6;2,7

The Meadow Pipit, like the Tree Pipit, sings a series of short songs from a perch, before launching into a song-flight; but the Meadow Pipit is usually perched on the ground, or on a low shrub, and the short songs are usually just a series of repeated notes 'tchee, tchee, tchee..' or such-like, and are continued as the bird ascends to the zenith of the song-flight. Then as the bird descends, it breaks into a series of varied phrases, less exuberant than the Tree Pipit, often repetitions of various notes, but incorporating some trilling and slowing of the tempo (2,6). Calls include a short, rattling trill and an abrupt 'chip, chi-chip', similar to the thin, 'tseep' call of an anxious bird (2,7). In the breeding season, Meadow Pipits appear very vocal, calling frequently when not singing. At other times usually heard calling in flight.

### Rock Pipit   *Anthus petrosus*   2,95

Rock Pipits are fairly vocal birds and have a similar vocabulary and song structure to the Meadow Pipit; but the Rock Pipit's voice is stronger, more metallic sounding and the song notes have a slightly trilled timbre. The full song is usually given in flight and often incorporates a buzzing trill. A repeated, terse 'tsip' call is frequently heard and a longer, more shrill 'tseep' from an anxious bird; the latter along with some chattering calls are heard when a bird becomes more alarmed.

### Yellow Wagtail   *Motacilla flava*   1,44

Yellow Wagtails have quite a variety of call notes mostly based around a slightly trilled 'tseu', 'sree' or a wheezy 'zwee', rising in pitch. A singing bird may use any of these calls repeated often in a slightly elongated and doubled form (1,44). Males make low undulating song-flights and deliver short but vigorous twittering songs, some sounding like a Swallow, amalgamated out of the call notes. The flight call is a rich 'zweep'.

### Grey Wagtail   *Motacilla cinerea*   2,61

Most often heard is the flight call as a bird passes above in its undulating flight - a loud, ringing 'tcheu-tcheu', similar in form to the Pied Wagtail's 'chissik', but more clearly given as two notes. Birds call and sing with similar repeated notes, a sibilant 'si-si-si' or a 'seu-seu-seu', sometimes developing a slight elaboration; the singing bird may be perched by the waterside or in a more prominent position, but frequently also in an undulating display flight down a river. Occasionally a male breaks into a more intense song, made up of a series of rich trills, reminiscent of a Chaffinch or a Wren. Birds call in flight throughout the year, but tend to sing mostly between April and July.

### Pied Wagtail   *Motacilla alba*   1,10

The Pied Wagtail is frequently heard giving its strident, disyllabic 'chissik' flight-call; often birds spend long periods delivering a series of variations on similar call notes, sometimes developing a phrase into a brief, subdued warble. Birds are quite vocal all year round but more so in the Spring and Autumn. In Spring males are occasionally heard to sing a more intense, but not loud, passage of warblings and trillings with a slightly scratchy quality to the voice. Birds gathered for Winter roosts can be very vocal, when the bushes seem to come alive with soft, warbled calls.

# WAXWINGS - BOMBYCILLIDAE

**Waxwing**    *Bombycilla garrulus*
The most frequently heard call is a fairly distinctive bell-like trilling, not loud, and reminiscent of a Grasshopper Warbler's reeling, but thinner and with a sibilance to it. Flocks can be quite vocal, but the calls are not heard easily at any distance. Birds sing with a regular repetition of a similar sibilant trill, but in a slightly fuller voice.

## DIPPERS - CINCLIDAE

**Dipper**    *Cinclus cinclus*                                                         2,60
Despite the hours of silence as it sits preening on some mid-stream rock, or hunts the stream bed with a series of underwater dives, the Dipper can be quite a vociferous bird. In flight it calls frequently a 'zip, zip' at intervals. Its song is often overlooked and aesthetically under-rated, blending with, yet standing out from the sound of running water. Its form is a leisurely warble of chirping and chacking notes, delivered in anything from short bursts to lengthy sustained passages, the notes flowing at a steady, regular rhythm. Birds can be heard singing all year round, though it is possibly at its quietest in late spring with the hard business of rearing young. Hearing a dipper in song can prove a real highlight of a mid-winter walk by a northern stream. I have been told of birds gathering in groups and indulging in a kind of communal subsong. And remember, its voice has evolved to the backdrop of running water.

## WRENS - TROGLODYTIDAE

**Wren**    *Troglodytes troglodytes*                                    1,20;1,76;1,95
The ubiquitous and vociferous Wren can be heard singing in virtually any habitat at any time of the year. The song is quite stereotyped in 4 to 5 second bursts, each consisting in a series of high-pitched trills and rapidly repeated notes, often with a marked sibilance (1,20;1,95). The powerful delivery, with body and wings quivering, seems beyond the physical proportions of the bird. At certain times of the day in the latter half of the year, the wrens may be the only birds singing in a woodland; then they sound like the real owners of the wood. Also frequently heard are the Wren's alarm calls, irregularly repeated sharp 'chak's and a rattling 'churr', which sounds like the 'chak's run together (1,76). A soft warbling subsong is sometimes heard from paired birds.

## DUNNOCKS - PRUNELLIDAE

**Dunnock**   *Prunella modularis*                                    1,16;1,18
The song of the Dunnock is a 2 to 3 second burst, with a similar
structure to the wren's - a series of trills and warbles at a slightly hurried
tempo and an even, quite loud level, but at a lower pitch and often with
less distinct phrases (1,18). Song is heard occasionally throughout the
year, but becomes more frequent from fine mornings in January through
to the Summer. In the early Spring a very beautiful subsong, soft and
liquid warbling, can sometimes be heard from within a bush or hedge-
row. Calls frequently with a plaintive sounding 'seep' (1,16), which can
vary from a slightly shrill pipe, especially when heard close, to a purer,
soft bleat. Also calls softly with a tremulous version of the above, almost
a trill.

## THRUSHES AND CHATS - TURDIDAE

This family of passerines has large eyes and are active early and late in
the day; they are usually the first wave of the dawn chorus. They are also
generally very vocal, with many species common and widespread in our
area. Although not strictly birds of open habitats, apart from the
Wheatear, most species can be found across a wide range of habitats.
Generally ground feeders they are essentially birds of open woodland
and the woodland edge, where trees and scrub offer relative security and
where birds tend to sing from more or less prominent perches. The
Nightingale singing in the quiet of the night can get away with singing
from the depths of a bush and still manage to broadcast his song. The
chats, tending to more open habitats, sing from lower song posts and
frequently make short, more or less vertical song-flights. In all species
full song is semi-stereotyped: it is given in fairly regular runs at even
intervals, each run generally conforming to an overall pattern, but made
up of varying phrases.

**Robin**   *Erithacus rubecula*                                    1,10;1,48
The song and calls of the Robin must be some of the most frequently
heard sounds in a number of habitats from the gardens of suburbia to
the dense conifer plantations of the uplands, even to the centre of cities.
With its sweet, wistful song the Robin is a likely source of the legendary
'Nightingale in Berkeley Square', as birds, stimulated by the street lights,
can often be heard singing in cities during the night. Vocal all year
round, song too is quite frequent throughout the year with a brief break
during moulting around July. Each song is around 3 to 6 seconds long,

differing from the previous one, and consisting of a mixture of fast warbled notes and some elongated slurred notes, with a wide pitch range (1,10). Birds sing at any time of the day, but Robins are often the first to sing at dawn and last at dusk. A repeated, sharp, high 'tic' call is frequently heard which turns into more of a series of rattling 'chk's if a bird becomes anxious (1,48). Also gives a thin, metallic 'tseep' and fuller 'tcheck's.

**Nightingale**  *Luscinia megarhynchos*  2,21
The Nightingale has acquired almost legendary status as a singer, partly through the rich exuberance of its song and partly through often being the only bird singing in the still quiet of the night. But not every bird singing at night is a Nightingale; depending on where you are it could be a Sedge Warbler or a Robin and Nightingales also sing by day. The Nightingale sings in fairly loud, 3 to 5 second bursts at short intervals, often for long periods; the song is distinguished by the ringing, clear tone of many of the notes, the rapid bursts of repeated notes with precision timing and the usual introduction to each song of a building series of softer notes. Often includes elements like 'jug-jug-jug...' or 'chook-chook-chook...' and may include some mimicry; some birds frequently have very high-pitched harmonics to some of their notes. Birds usually sing from thick cover, but occasionally from a more exposed perch; song is heard mostly from late April to early June. Calls include a warbler-like 'hweet', quite a deep churring note 'krrr' and chat-like chakking notes.

**Bluethroat**  *Luscinia svecica*
The song of the Bluethroat has more variation than the Nightingale, but lacks the ringing clarity of the latter's voice, sounding closer to the warblers, often with much mimicry. Also distinguished by a wheezing tone to many phrases, a high metallic overtone to some notes and the inclusion of some liquid, rippling trills. Like the Nightingale, calls include a sweet, but short 'weet' and chat-like 'chakk's.

**Black Redstart**  *Phoenicurus ochruros*
The male's song is a short burst (usually less than a second) of scratchy warbling given at short intervals; usually not as fast a warble as the Whitethroat. Displaying birds also produce chattering 'churr's, not unlike a Magpie, but in a lighter voice. Calls include a short, high-pitched 'seep' and repeated, chacking 'tch's.

**Redstart**  *Phoenicurus phoenicurus*                                    1,77

The male Redstart delivers his songs at regular intervals, each lasting from around 2 to 4 seconds, usually from a high perch in a tree. Almost every song begins with the same couple of phrases, which may vary in different regions, but in Britain tends to be a Chaffinch-like 'hooee-hyu-hyu-hyu-hyu....'; this is followed by a warbled passage, often including bill-clicking and mimicry, which is varied in each subsequent song. Many find this song dull, but for me it is a model of under-stated precision; and a bird singing in courtship to a female nearby, delivers an almost continuous, varied warble, including some very odd notes like metallic buzzes and 'zing's. Song can be heard from around the middle of April to the end of June, at any time of the day, and, where they are plentiful, Redstarts are often singing at dawn before even the Robins and Blackbirds. The most frequently heard calls are a Willow Warbler-like 'hwee' and a sharp, thin, repeated 'tic' or 'tch', often together from an anxious bird.

**Winchat**  *Saxicola rubetra*                                    2,3;2,4

The Winchat, like the Redstart and Stonechat, sings most intensely very early in the morning. Each song is a short burst of 1 or 2 seconds, with a short interval before the next, usually delivered from the top of a bush, occasionally in a brief 'song-flutter'; in form it is typically a scratchy warble, often containing rattling trills, chacking notes and purer tones, but some birds can be superb mimics - those in Northern Britain frequently producing Grey Partridge calls (2,3). Song is heard from when the birds arrive in mid April through to early July. Calls include a short, flutey 'phew' and repeated, hard, abrupt 'tchk's, usually heard together from an anxious bird (2,4).

**Stonechat**  *Saxicola torquata*                                    1,50;1,51

As mentioned above, Stonechats tend to sing most intensely very early in the morning, usually from the top of gorse bush or telephone wire, sometimes in a vertical, bouncing song-flight. The song is similar in form to the Winchat (also the Wheatear and Dartford Warbler, for that matter), delivered in short bursts at short intervals and is likewise a fast warble (1,50). But, compared to the Winchat, the song is more hurried, is more uniform with less marked phrasing, lacks the rattling trills and has a thinner, high-pitched voice with more of a whistling tone to it. Song can be heard from March through to around mid July. Calls include a rattling 'chack' and a thin, high 'weet', usually delivered by an anxious bird at an intruder (1,51).

**Wheatear**   *Oenanthe oenanthe*                                    2,10

The Wheatear's song is a short burst of scratchy warbling like the above two species, delivered at a tempo similar to the Stonechat, but in a voice closer to the Winchat, including chacking or churring sounds. It may be given from the ground or in a short song-flight; subsequent songs are varied, with short intervals between. Males sing from very early in the morning and then on and off through the day, sometimes in poor weather conditions; they sing from when they begin to arrive in March through to early July, but song is most intense early on and becomes more sporadic in June. Calls include terse, hard 'chak's and thin, short 'see's or 'weet's, usually heard from an anxious bird.

**Ring Ouzel**   *Turdus torquatus*                                   2,8;2,9

Ring Ouzels are quite wary birds living in what is generally an open habitat and are most often heard calling anxiously, having seen you approaching from a distance. Alarm calls are repeated single notes, 'tchukk', and a longer rattle like the blackbird, but in an explosive, chacking voice (2,9 after the Peregrine). Males are most often heard singing a basic form of their song, three single or sometimes double flutey notes which carry well; this is repeated at regular intervals which may be quite long (2,8). But excited birds, possibly when the female is close by, sing a fuller version including quieter, Song Thrush-like warbled motifs. Song can be heard from mid March through to mid June and sometimes later.

**Blackbird**   *Turdus merula*                                       1,4;1,7

Blackbirds are quite vocal pretty well throughout the year; males sing on brighter days in the late Winter and more persistently from the early Spring through to July, sometimes resuming again in the Autumn. At other times birds can be heard calling repeatedly, particularly around their roosts in the morning and evening; they also call occasionally while foraging, often as a pair or in a small group, and readily call in alarm. Each song is typically 2 to 3 seconds long with a similar interval before the next, and consists of a warbled series of notes beginning strong and flutey, ending with faster scratchy notes (1,4). Birds have quite a wide repertoire of phrases, with certain motifs becoming established on a regional basis, and individual birds developing preferences for characteristic phrases. Individuals also have regular song-posts, so it can be quite easy to get to know individual birds. Song can be particularly mellifluous, and sometimes includes mimicry, usually when a male is excited and courting a female nearby. Blackbirds sing their first songs in the early dawn and in many habitats the first wave of the dawn chorus is made up of Blackbirds and Robins. Song is occasional through the day and often more frequent again in the evening. When disturbed, birds frequently give a distinctive rattling call of variable phrasing, as they fly off. In general behaviour birds often call with soft, clucking 'chuck's, which become more intense 'spink's, rapidly repeated, when a bird is anxious (1,7).

**Fieldfare**   *Turdus pilaris*                                                    1,69
For much of the time Fieldfares are quite vocal birds; a fairly continuous chatter of single 'chak's and little chuckling motifs, in a voice not unlike the Ring Ouzel, is heard from flocks in Autumn, Winter and Spring, both feeding and in flight and especially around a roost. Generally breeding in colonies, territorial song is less important for Fieldfares and song is occasional, consisting in a passage of subsong-like warbling, often breaking out of or accompanied by the more usual calling. It is not in as loud a voice as the chattering calls and does not carry far. Communal singing is sometimes heard from migrating flocks in the Spring.

**Song Thrush**   *Turdus philomelos*                              1,93;1,58
Song Thrushes can be fairly quiet birds for much of the time, but males in song are audibly conspicuous. Song is heard occasionally through the Winter, but begins in earnest early in the new year, sometimes in January in southern regions. Song is loud, varied and with a distinct tendency for rhythmic repetition of phrases; often notes are short, clear and powerful, but can include high-pitched, wheezy warblings, especially as Summer comes on (1,93). Song can be heard at any time of the day, frequently early and late, but often birds do not begin singing until the Blackbirds and Robins have been going for a little while and maybe the Wrens have started up. Alarmed birds call readily with bursts of a rapidly repeated, sharp chacking 'tsk-tsk-tsk....', distinctive and often mimicked by other species in song (1,58). In more general situations calls include a quieter, clucking 'tchuk' and sometimes a thin 'tsee'

**Redwing**   *Turdus iliacus*                                                   1,96
The Redwing is quite a vocal species though birds feeding individually can be silent. The song of the Redwing, though not outstandingly pretty, is very interesting. Breeding males sing a stereotyped song of several slightly trilled or flutey notes from fairly prominent perches. This is a regularly repeated motif which clearly varies with different geographical populations; this is maybe all that is delivered. But, rather like the Ring Ouzel, there is another part to the song, a kind of subsong

which is usually given with the main song as an ending: this is a varied warbling, like a frantic chattering, in a quieter voice, and may be sustained for quite long passages (1,96). This kind of singing, without the stereotyped part of the song, is sometimes heard sung communally from migrating flocks in the Spring. The usual contact call is a liquid 'twip' and a sharper 'tchik', which becomes a more Fieldfare-like 'tchack' when a bird is alarmed or excited. Frequently calls with a quite loud, very high-pitched, slightly shrill 'seee', like a predator warning call in other species, but which here seems to be used for general contact, especially in flight.

**Mistle Thrush**   *Turdus viscivorus*                                1,23;1,90
The song of the Mistle Thrush is closer to the Blackbird than the Song Thrush; it lacks the formal repetition of the latter's song and is closer in tone to the Blackbird (1,90). Songs are often delivered with very little interval between them; each consists of a warbled series of notes in a full whistling voice, at a quicker tempo than the Blackbird's. The main part of the song is usually very melodic to our ears, but there may be a hurried more scratchy ending, similar to a Blackbird's ending. Song is usually delivered from a high perch and birds begin singing early in the year, around January, often on wild, but bright days - hence its colloquial name, Stormcock. By May song is less frequent, but can be heard again occasionally in the Autumn. The drawn-out, irregular rattling alarm call is distinctive and frequently heard (1,23).

# WARBLERS - SYLVIIDAE

Living in fairly dense vegetation as most warbler species do, there is a limit to the effectiveness of visual signalling for longer distance communication (note that some of the open habitat species indulge in little song flights, often vertically from a perch, to get noticed). As an adaptation to this constraint on visual communication, the warblers, as their name suggests, have developed song to a high degree, rather than plumage; in generally they appear as classic 'little brown jobs'. Those species which enjoy the relative security of the densest vegetation are able to sing fairly continuous songs. There is a suggestion that song has more of a courtship than territorial function in some species, since the males sing less once they have acquired a mate. Most species call in alarm with various terse 'tchack's or short churring, buzzy calls.

**Cetti's Warbler**   *Cettia cetti*
Cetti's Warblers sing in brief explosive bursts with fairly long intervals

between them - often 15 to 20 seconds and sometimes longer; and they usually manage to slip unseen to another spot for subsequent deliveries. Each song is suprisingly loud and consists mainly in a repeated phrase, often 'chu, chuwee-chuwee-chuwee-chuwee', but indivuals have their own phrases which can be more complex. Song can be heard at any time of the year, but mainly from early Spring to early Summer, with some resumption in the Autumn; birds sometimes sing at night. Calls include a sharp 'teck'.

**Grasshopper Warbler**   *Locustella naevia*                    2,28;2,33

In common with several other *Locustella* warblers, the 'reeling' song of the 'Gropper' resembles the stridulation of an insect more than a bird song. It is a fast, slightly metallic, buzzing trill, often kept up for long passages with the briefest of breaks; individual bursts can be anything up to several minutes long and birds have been known to sing for up to 4 hours in a session. Singing birds turn their heads slowly from side to side, so the sound drifts and is quite difficult to locate. Song is heard most frequently at dusk and dawn, and often through the night, from when the males arrive in late April or early May, through to July when it becomes more occasional. Males also tend to sing less persistently once paired. Birds sing well on warm, humid nights and on a calm night can be heard at up to four hundred metres.

**Savi's Warbler**   *Locustella luscinioides*

The song of the Savi's Warbler is of the same form as the Grasshopper Warbler, but lower-pitched and usually delivered in shorter bursts. Tonally the notes are more of a click and lack the metallic ring of the Gropper, but are delivered with the same swinging head movement. Song is heard in the breeding season usually between April and July.

**Sedge Warbler**   *Acrocephalus schoenobaenus*                    2,22;2,27

Each song of the male Sedge Warbler tends to last from around 30 seconds to 1 minute, and sometimes longer. Typically a song begins with some chirring chirps, quite grating in tone, at a brisker tempo than the Reed Warbler, but to an erratic rhythm. As the song builds up steam, as it were, the buzzing rhythms are interspersed with 'ti-ti-ti...'s and passages of quick-fire mimicry. Song is usually delivered from the top of tall herbage or a small bush, sometimes in a short, fluttering song-flight or deeper in vegetation. Males begin singing persistently from when they arrive in late April, but singing becomes more sporadic, mainly in the early morning, once a bird is paired; unpaired birds continue to sing frequently during the day and often at night through till the end of July, when they sing only occasionally. Their most commonly heard calls are a sharp 'tuk', often repeated and given in alarm, and a slow, grating churr, low-pitched and with a slightly hollow sound.

## Marsh Warbler   *Acrocephalus palustris*

The Marsh Warbler is one of the most vibrant singers of Northern Europe; song is in sustained passages of fast warbling, full of expert mimicry, with the sounds of House Sparrows, Swallows, Linnets and Blue Tits often featured. In voice, the churring tones of the Sedge and Reed Warblers are occasionally detectable, but there are many more liquid notes, trills and much more versatility than either of those two species; nevertheless individuals vary and a poor singer or a less vigorous performance later in the season can be less easy to distinguish as a Marsh Warbler. Males sing for a short period in early summer, the first heard around late May and the last in early July, often from a fairly high perch. Calls include a hard 'tic' varying to a 'tchuck' and a high-pitched churring note or rattle, similar to, but not so harsh as the Sedge Warbler, in alarm.

## Reed Warbler   *Acrocephalus scirpaceus*                                    2,23

Like the other two *Acrocephalus* warblers, the Reed Warbler often sings in long sustained passages, but to a regular, throbbing rhythm at a steady tempo; songs are typically made up of short repetitions of various notes like 'jug-jug-jug-chirruc-chirruc...' in a churring voice, less hard and buzzy than the Sedge Warbler and at a fairly constant, lower pitch. Some birds are prone to mimic, but mimicked calls are rarely as frequent as with the Sedge or Marsh Warblers. Males sing usually from within their dense reed-beds, from arrival in late April; song becomes less frequent through July to occasional in August. The usual call is a low churr, which may be lengthened to a grating rattle, similar to but faster than the Sedge, as a bird becomes more alarmed.

## Dartford Warbler   *Sylvia undata*                                    1,49;1,52

The song of the Dartford Warbler is a short, fast, scratchy warble usually delivered at short intervals and reminiscent of both the Stonechat and the Whitethroat; but compared to the Dartford Warbler's harsh, churring tone, giving a fast chattering impression, these species have clear voices (1,49). Each song burst lasts from 1 to 1.5 seconds and features very fast melodic patterns with quite a wide pitch range, incorporating several high-pitched whistling notes. Song can be heard on occasions at any time of the year, but is most frequent between March and June and very early on sunny mornings. Birds usually sing from low perches, occasionally from higher song-posts and often in short, vertical song-flights. The usual call, heard from an anxious bird, is a hard, metallic 'tchirr', with a distinct nasal tone to it rather like the Whitethroat (1,52); also a sharp 'tucc'.

### Lesser Whitethroat   *Sylvia curruca*                              1,40
The Lesser Whitethroat's song is in the form of a passing warble introducing a rattling trill, each song lasting less than 2 seconds, delivered at intervals of around 5 to 10 seconds; in some birds the warble is very short, but can be of a more substantial length in others. The fairly distinctive trill, though often described as rattling, resembles an elongated phrase in a Chaffinch song and can be easily missed where there are Chaffinches about. Song is usually delivered from a fairly prominent perch, such as the top of a shrub, and is heard mainly through May and June. Usual calls are a hard, repeated 'tchik' (typical of *Sylvia* warblers) and a low, buzzy churr like that of the Whitethroat, but not so harsh.

### Whitethroat   *Sylvia communis*                              1,33;1,36
The song of the Whitethroat is a hurried, slightly scratchy warble, given at short intervals, with quite a pleasant, chirping quality to the voice (1,33). Often subsequent songs feature the same introductory note or phrase, at least when singing from a perch in cover; songs delivered in a vertical, fluttering flight tend to be more varied, longer and more elaborate. Birds sing from when they are arriving in their breeding areas in April through to July when song becomes less frequent. Calls are a short, harsh churr and a sharp 'tack', usually from an alarmed pair (1,36).

### Garden Warbler   *Sylvia borin*                              1,26
Now we come to the difficult two - the Garden Warbler and the Blackcap. The males of both species often sing from within a bush or tree obscured by foliage and they have very similar songs to our ears. The songs of both are an extended, liquid warble, though the Garden Warbler frequently sings some long passages without a break, sometimes over 1 minute, which is rare in the Blackcap - unless it is in subsong. I have found the most reliable distinguishing characteristics to be the steady, hurried rhythm of the Garden Warbler's delivery, a bubbling or slightly trilling quality to the voice and the lack of pure, flutey, or Blackbird-like notes; the Garden Warbler also frequently delivers passages in a kind of wheezing falsetto voice. Song is heard at any time of the day, but especially in the early morning from late April to early July, when it becomes more occasional. Some birds, probably unmated males sing very persistently. The usual calls are a sharp 'teck',

which are rapidly repeated in runs as a bird becomes more alarmed, and, less frequently, a quieter, raspy churr, both typical of the *Sylvia* warblers.

**Blackcap**   *Sylvia atricapilla*                                              1,28
Whereas the Garden Warbler sings an even, hurried warble with a uniformity of phrasing, the Blackcap sings with more distinct melodic phrases, varying the tempo and usually including some rich, pure notes. Also songs vary much more between individual males (to our ears), with some individuals developing 'signature' tunes. Song-bursts are usually around 5 seconds long, but occasionally individuals may sing very long passages of several minutes without a break. Whereas each song-burst of the Garden Warbler tends to peter out or just come to a stop, the Blackcap's song often has a distinct, full-voiced ending, usually with a rising flourish. Nevertheless birds are frequently heard in subsong, which tends to be more hurried, with more scratchy phrases, much of it at a high pitch and lacking the full, pure notes, hence sounding in some ways more like a Garden Warbler (in 1,28 the bird is singing intensely with elements of subsong); furthermore mimicry is quite frequent in the Blackcap, including mimicry of Garden Warbler song passages. With much experience it is usually possible to distinguish the two species by song, but visual identification always helps. The usual call is a hard 'tak', close to the similar call of the Lesser Whitethroat, heard from excited or anxious birds, and a churr similar to the Garden Warbler when alarmed.

**Wood Warbler**   *Phylloscopus sibilatrix*                        1,82;1,84
The song of the Wood Warbler is virtually unmistakable; no other species in our region produces such an accomplished, ecstatic trill. Males sing throughout the day, most frequently in the morning and probably again in the evening, as they move through the trees under the canopy feeding (1,82). The song begins with a few repeated 'tsic' notes, gradually accelerating into a rapid trill, the singer overcome with quivering wings, before the notes come to an end fairly abruptly; the whole song lasts 2 to 3 seconds and is repeated at intervals, but is rarely given twice from the same spot. It is frequently delivered in a fluttering flight between two trees. The song is often accompanied by a series of sweet, almost disyllabic 'tyeu' notes (1,84). Alarmed birds call with a more monosyllabic version of this call, but with the same sweet timbre. Song is heard from the end of April to the end of June and occasionally in July.

**Chiffchaff**   *Phylloscopus collybita*                                    1,67
The male's song from which the bird gets its name is a series of 'chiff'
and 'chaff' notes delivered at a steady, relaxed tempo, but not always
sounding like the two-note 'chiff-chaff'; it is quite loud and carries well.
This is delivered at intervals, usually like the other *Phylloscopus* warblers
as the bird is moving through the trees feeding. The song usually lasts
between about 4 and 8 seconds and is often preceded by a softer,
scratchy 'tirric'-like note (1,67). Birds arrive back in their breeding areas
quite early and song can often be heard from the end of March through
to July when it becomes more occasional; there is a slight resumption in
passage in early Autumn. The usual call heard is a Willow Warbler-like
'hwee', but more of a single rising note, given by anxious birds.

**Willow Warbler**   *Phylloscopus trochilus*                          1,78;1,81
Visually very difficult to distinguish from the Chiffchaff, the song of the
Willow Warbler is unmistakable and is redolent of Spring through much
of our region. It is a melodious warble consisting in a rippling series of
sweet 'hwee', 'teu' and such-like notes, run together and gradually
descending in pitch (1,81). Each song lasts usually no more than 2 to 3
seconds with short intervals between songs when birds are singing
intensely and often longer intervals of 30 seconds or more later in the
Summer. Song can be heard from the beginning of April through to
July, when it becomes less frequent. Like the Chiffchaff there is some
resumption of song from birds on passage in the early Autumn. Frequent calls include  a plaintive 'tuu' 'hoo-ee', more disyllabic than the
Chiffchaff, from anxious birds (1,78), and several thin, buzzy alarm
calls, one of which is particularly used when a Cuckoo is about.

**Goldcrest**   *Regulus regulus*                                            1,91
Goldcrests are really quite vocal birds; they begin to sing earnestly in the
early Spring, often on fine days in February. Early songs are often a
loose, but quite loud kind of subsong; by April full song is the norm. It
is fairly stereotyped and very thin and high-pitched, consisting in a
'tee-le-dee' type motif of slightly squeaky notes, repeated several times
fairly rapidly, leading to a terminal flourish, often incorporating a little
trill. With several birds singing in close proximity, the individual songs
merge into a general sibilance. Song is frequent through to July when it
becomes more sporadic, and is resumed again through the Autumn.
Goldcrests call frequently in contact with each other with repeated,
high-pitched 'tsee's; and these range from very soft, Blue Tit-like notes
to much stronger, but still thin, slightly trilled notes.

**Firecrest**  *Regulus ignicapillus*
The Firecrest has a very similar thin, high-pitched voice to the Goldcrest
and on first hearing the song sounds very similar too. But it is simpler,
being little more than an accelerating series of repeated 'tsee' or 'zit'
notes without any distinct motif; there is also no real flourish at the end,
though there may be a hint of a motif in the introductory phrase of the
song. It is generally shorter than the Goldcrest's song, usually around 2
seconds to the Goldcrest's 3 to 4. Song is most frequent in May and
June, particularly after dawn; after that it becomes less frequent, usually
heard only in the morning. The usual contact call is a 'zit-zit-zit',
harsher and slightly lower than the similar calls of the Goldcrest.

## FLYCATCHERS - MUSCICAPIDAE

**Spotted Flycatcher**  *Muscicapa striata*                                    1,83
It is not easy to recognie a male Spotted Flycatcher's full song as distinct
from its usual calls; essentially a singing bird 'plays' with the call notes.
The male also gives a quieter, excited kind of subsong, which can be
intense in courtship; odd phrases from this type of song may occur in
the more territorial type of song. The basic contact call is a thin,
high-pitched, squeaking trill around a 'tsee'; this is repeated frequently
at short intervals, often a few seconds, each call being varied slightly.
Singing birds increase the variation and in subsong deliver a high,
squeaky warbling in a similar voice. Generally quite vocal though easily
missed because of the high pitched voice and the continual movement of
the birds, they can be heard often from May to July then go a bit quieter;
song only tends to be heard in the early part of the breeding season,
certainly the subsong element. Anxious birds call with a quite hard,
churring chack, usually in runs of two or three.

**Pied Flycatcher**  *Ficedula hypoleuca*                                      1,72
The most basic version of the Pied Flycatcher's song is a series of
around 5 or 6 distinctly enunciated notes, delivered at a steady tempo,
often with a hint of a simple melody; such a song might easily sound
something like 'chi-chew-chu, chi-chew-chi', at a slightly quicker pace
than a Chiffchaff, and subsequent songs often feature only slight variation and can sound monotonously similar. But there is wide variation in
individual birds' repertoires. Often warbling phrases occur; and some
individuals have beautifully melodic motifs which work almost like a
signature tune for that bird (to our ears). Males sing frequently on

arrival in their breeding areas; once birds have paired singing becomes rare. Calls include a sharp 'wit'.

# TIMALIIDAE

**Bearded Tit**   *Panurus biarmicus*                                    2,25
Bearded Tits are generally quite vocal birds, as individuals in a small party call to keep in contact; with increased flocking activity in the Autumn, birds are probably at their most vocal. Calling is based around variations of a distinctive 'pyew' note, usually described as pings from the slightly metallic ringing tone to many of the notes; several other calls are sometimes heard. Song has been described as a twittering rattle, but is not often heard. Calls and vocal behaviour bear some similarity to the Long-tailed Tit.

# AEGITHALIDAE

**Long-tailed Tit**   *Aegithalos caudatus*                               1,74
Whether a breeding pair or in a flock, Long-tailed Tits are rarely silent for long. A winter flock can liven up an otherwise silent woodland, as the birds maintain contact with a variety of fairly soft, high-pitched calls; a large flock, often with a few other species keeping company, can often be heard at some distance - possibly several hundred yards in calm conditions. The three most commonly heard calls are a high 'see', sometimes emphatically trilled and often given as a triplet 'see-see-see', a terse 'chrrp' and a soft 'tupp'. Song is a slightly more elaborate working of variations on the calls, but is not often heard.

# TITS - PARIDAE

The species of this family, and to a certain extent the Long-tailed Tit, are generally very vocal, both in their breeding seasons and in the other months when the different species often band together in mixed flocks; but they can prove very difficult to distinguish through their general contact calls, which are mostly thin, high-pitched notes and soft trills. The species of the *Parus* genus have quite extensive vocabularies of different calls and the repertoires of individuals usually contain various songs and various renditions of the call motifs. Most of these species have churring or rattling alarm calls, which with their variation can be quite difficult to distinguish. To confuse matters further some of the species, particularly the Great Tit, seem prone to mimic the calls of the other closely related species. Females of this genus are heard to sing occasionally - but it is rarely possible to tell the sex of a bird of these species. These species tend to be residential in their haunts throughout the year and song, along with the establishment of territories and pairing, begins early in the year.

**Marsh Tit**   *Parus palustris*                                                              1,64
The Marsh Tit is probably best known vocally from its 'pi-tchew' call, which may be extended into a 'pi-tchuwuwuwu' or 'pi-tchaweeu'; this can sound quite similar to some Coal Tit songs, but the 'pi' of the first syllable has a distinctive ringing tone to it in the Marsh Tit. This call is heard throughout the year. Contact calls are thin, high notes, often soft. The male's usual song is formally simple - a single, rich note repeated quickly in a series of 5 or 6; the notes are harmonically precise, again with a distinct tone and each descending slightly in pitch. Birds usually have other motifs with which they sing, often using variants of the 'p-tchew' call. Song is heard most frequently in the early Spring, from February to April, and occasionally in the Winter months.

**Willow Tit**   *Parus montanus*                                                           1,66
The most characteristic sounds of the Willow Tit are a descending, plaintive 'tsew', repeated several times in succession, and a nasal, churring 'tchaayy'. The former acts as a kind of territorial call or song and is far-carrying; its form and rhythm, at a steadier pace than the swiftly-repeated song note of the Marsh Tit, is similar to the Nuthatch's 'hui-hui-hui...' song, but that rises in pitch. Birds can be quite vocal at times, but seem to be less sociable than the other tit species. Song can be heard at any time of year, but most frequently from late Winter through the Spring and again from late Summer into the Autumn. A softer warbling and trills are sometimes given and females sing occasionally. Other calls include thin 'zee-zee's, various motifs on similar notes and a churring alarm call, all confusingly similar to a Blue Tit, but generally with a more nasal tone of voice.

**Crested Tit**   *Parus cristatus*                                                          1,89
Crested Tits call frequently with a variety of high-pitched, thin, often slightly trilled whistles, not unlike a Long-tailed Tit, but sharper and often given in little rhythmic motifs; these are frequently interspersed with a distinctive, slightly rattling, purring trill. Song tends to be a more intense working of the call notes and themes and can be heard at most times of year, but most frequently in the Spring.

**Coal Tit** *Parus ater*                                                   1,97
The Coal Tit has quite a wide vocabulary of calls and there is much
variation in songs. Calls include a plaintive, descending 'teu', less
slurred than the similar call of the Siskin, similar notes like 'tee' and a
rising 'tooee', a high 'quee-quee-quee' and various thin, scratchy, trilling
alarm calls. Songs are often see-sawing, double-note chimes like the
Great Tit, but thinner, higher-pitched and often given at a brisker
tempo. A vocal bird for much of the year, family parties in the Summer
can be vociferous, though song is most frequent in the Spring.

**Blue Tit** *Parus caeruleus*                              1,8;1,61;1,62
Foraging for food in a small party or a flock, Blue Tits call readily in
contact with soft, thin 'see-see' notes; the alarm churr, often rising in
pitch to a rattling ending, is frequently heard (1,62) and a variety of
other calls used on occasions, many based around slightly squeaky or
scratchy trilled notes. Song can be heard at any time of year, but is most
frequent from late Winter to early Summer; birds usually have several
song types in their repertoires (1,62), but the commonest types are
variations on 'seee-seee-see-chu-chu-chu-chu', often with the ending
trilled (1,8). Birds also sing with a sustained, sibilant trilling in courtship, often leading up to mating.

**Great Tit** *Parus major*                    1,15;1,16;1,24;1,63;1,64
Though occasionally quieter than some of the other tit species while
going about their general business, Great Tits call readily, and often
aggressively, in alarm and often become very vocal, particularly in
Spring, with wide and varied vocabularies. Most characteristically,
Great Tits sing with precise, but simple, repeated motifs; the most
frequent form of song has often been described as a chiming 'tea-cher,
tea-cher...', but there are many slight variations and individuals usually
have a variety of songs which may include some with more complicated
3 or 4 note patterns (1,15;1,24;1;64 after Marsh Tit song). All songs
tend to be in a characteristically chiming voice conveyed by the precise
harmonics of the notes: the formal simplicity of many of the songs
should not be taken as a measure of the Great Tit's vocal skills - they are
the vehicle for notes of great tonal beauty. Great Tits also give a wide
variety of calls including confusing imitations of other tit species. A
Chaffinch-like, repeated 'spink' is often heard and the alarm churr, often
preceeded by an abrupt, whistled 'see', has more of a hollow rattle to it
than the Blue Tit (1,16 after Dunnock calls). Various calls based on
forceful whistled notes are also frequently heard, sometimes in complex

motifs, that are difficult to distinguish from songs (1,63). Full song is most frequent in the Spring with a resumption in the early Autumn.

## NUTHATCHES - SITTIDAE

**Nuthatch**    *Sitta europaea*                                           1,61
The Nuthatch is often a fairly vocal bird; with several very distinctive calls and quite unobtrusive habits, it is a useful species to learn to recognise vocally. Most characteristic is a single or repeated 'twoit', when a bird is slightly agitated, which becomes more strident when a bird is alarmed. Contact calls are soft, high, thin notes like the tit species, with whom Nuthatches regularly associate in Winter flocks. The male's song is a loud, rising 'twee' or 'hui' repeated in runs of around six. Birds also have a distinctive territorial call, a ringing steady trill. Song is most frequent from late Winter through Spring with a resumption in the early Autumn.

## TREECREEPERS - CERTHIIDAE

**Treecreeper**    *Certhia familiaris*                              1,67;1,75
Working their way up the bark of a tree, Treecreepers frequently call in contact with very soft 'see's, similar to the calls of Goldcrests and various tit species; nevertheless a useful indication of the bird's presence, since they can be quite elusive in their scurrying habits and low flights between trunks, even at close hand. More distinctive is a high-pitched, slightly shrill 'tseu', often given in a run of 2 or 3, used for longer distance contact (1,67 in the distance); again this is similar to calls of the Goldcrest and Long-tailed Tit, but the notes are more sustained and forceful. Song seems to be a stereotyped high-pitched warble, introduced by one or more trilled notes, usually descending in pitch to an ending flourish (1,75). Song is most frequent from late Winter to early Summer, with a slight resumption in the Autumn.

## ORIOLIDAE

**Golden Oriole**    *Oriolus oriolus*                                  1,55
Golden Orioles can be quite vocal birds and, with a fairly loud song and calls, sound is often the best clue to their presence hidden in a wood's foliage. Calls are a varied range of harsh sounds, from cat-like mewings to Jay-like squawks and Magpie-like chattering. The male's song is delivered as regular short warbles in a rich, flutey voice; motifs fre-

quently sound like 'weel-awee-oo' or 'too-lu-wee-oo' and is characteristically very melodious.

# SHRIKES - LANIIDAE

Shrikes, though silent for long periods can be quite vocal birds. Calls tend to be slightly harsh chatterings and explosive chaks, with a scratchy tone of voice; song tends to be an understated warble, often regarded as subsong, frequently including mimicry, with a mixture of harsh and sweeter sounds.

### Red-backed Shrike  *Lanius collurio*
Red-backed Shrikes sometimes sing in short passages in Winter, giving the impression of idly playing with sounds, but in Spring deliver sustained passages of warbling in the style of the Sylvia warblers. Song can be heard through to the early Summer, but apparently not all males sing and the sound does not carry far. Calls are varied with explosive 'tchak's given in alarm, intense short churrs and frequently copies of other species calls.

### Great Grey Shrike  *Lanius excubitor*
Calls tend to be harsh and vary from Starling-like wheezy churrs to restrained shrieks, reminiscent of a Jay. The male's song can be surprisingly sweet-voiced and may have a liquid warbled phrase suggesting, or in imitation of, a Golden Oriole's song; other phrases, often mimicking other species, sound harsher and bear more resemblance to the calling voice of the bird. Birds repeat phrases, usually based on imitations, at short intervals, sometimes with slight variations but often with identical renditions and the imitations have a particular tone, difficult to define, in common with other *Lanius* Shrikes.

# CROWS - CORVIDAE

The crow family tend to produce 'gutteral', croaking sounds and hence the word 'crow' or, as we say in Northumberland, 'craa'. They are a fairly vocal lot, as they are also quite social, with different species often associating together. Early on winter mornings a large wave of calling corvids passes over our village, as Rooks and Jackdaws leave their roosts in the woods together and head out to the farm fields to feed. Nevertheless individuals and groups of birds can be silent for long periods as they forage and hunt for food.

**Jay**   *Garrulus glandarius*                                                1,57
Jays often go about their business silently; when you disturb a bird, or a
pair, they almost always give their harsh, screeching call. Similar calls
can be heard from single birds and small groups establishing status, and
this can result in quite a clamour. More rarely, or rather more rarely
heard, birds produce softer cackling and croaking. This is sometimes
delivered as a sort of warbling song, often including mimicry.

**Magpie**   *Pica pica*                                                       1,27
Magpies generally reveal their presence with regular calling, with anything from single chacks to runs of chacking chatter. Their voice,
though tonally rough, does not have the screeching quality of the Jay.
Birds also often call in a softer, mewing voice and sometimes produce a
warbling song out of these softer calls.

**Chough**   *Pyrrhocorax pyrrhocorax*                                         2,96
The Chough's vocal behaviour is similar to their close relative, the
Jackdaw, with birds calling frequently in flight, often in small parties,
and around the breeding colony. Calls are varied, roughly similar to a
Jackdaw's, but less explosive and in a hoarser voice. A sharp 'kow', a
gruff, rolling 'kaarr' and a higher-pitched, more yelping 'kee-ah' are
frequently heard.

**Jackdaw**   *Corvus monedula*                                               1,14
Jackdaws tend to live in loose colonies and spend much of their time in
family parties or small flocks, often as part of a much larger mixed flock
of corvids. Rapid calling between birds breaks out frequently from both
perched birds and flying birds. Their voice is based on a croaky, strident
'jack' or 'tcheck', higher-pitched and more abrupt than the rook or
carrion crow. Calling can be varied as birds produce runs of notes,
varying the tone, pitch and rhythm of the phrase.

**Rook**   *Corvus frugilegus*                                             1,13;1,42
Rooks are as vocal as they are social. Nesting in colonies, often moving
about and feeding in flocks, their calls vary from soft, contact-type
croaking to loud, raucous cawing in status disputes and displays. The
voice of the rook is very similar to the Carrion Crow, but is less harsh,
with a more purring quality to it, and has more suggestion of a musical
pitch to it. In fact Rooks have developed an astonishing variety of
expressions from that apparently limited voice, ranging from croaky
rattles to crooning calls. Sometimes a single bird will be seen giving vent
with full voice from a prominent perch, with its tail spread and bobbing

its head down as it calls. Unexpectedly, a bird that repays time spent listening to it.

**Carrion/Hooded Crow**   *Corvus corone*                                    1,6;1,42
The north country 'craa' does indeed craa. Both Carrion and Hooded Crows are more solitary birds than most other corvids, nesting usually in isolated pairs, though they do spend some time foraging in small flocks or gangs. Birds call frequently perched or in flight with a harder-edged caw than the Rook (1,42 for comparison). The call is usually repeated several times in quick succession, and variations on the theme are fairly limited, but include some softer mewing caws. It is said that the voice of the Hooded Crow is deeper than that of the Carrion.

**Raven**   *Corvus corax*                                                  1,73;2,19
Ravens are generally quite vocal birds, particularly so in courtship and display in the Spring(1,73); breeding begins early with Ravens and birds can be at their most vociferous on fine days in January, when birds indulge in spectacular aerial displays. Birds often call at regular intervals in flight, even when passing over at a great height (2,19). Typical calls are a deep, resonant 'cronk', a variety of rhythmically rolling 'krra-krra-krra's, some in odd but musical tones of voice, and a sharp, ringing 'pruk'; but calls are very variable in this species and occasionally birds give short, chattering or almost warbled passages though in the Raven's deep voice. Birds typically repeat calls in short rhythmic series.

## STARLINGS - STURNIDAE

**Starling**   *Sturnus vulgaris*                                            1,3
Starlings are very vocal birds all year round and produce a wide range of sounds from pure loud whistles and harsh shrieks to soft, warbling chatter. Birds foraging in flocks, and especially at roosts, usually maintain a constant warbling chatter; occasionally disputes between individuals arise and a few louder, rattling shrieks are heard above the general bubbling. Birds sing, often in duets, from prominent perches - TV aerials are very popular. Singing birds usually give occasional varied whistles and other calls between bursts of frenzied warbling and chattering that may last anything up to a minute. This burst of song will usually include a series of repeated trilled whistles, runs of bill-clicking and precise imitations of the calls of several other species, as highlights in a constant, rhythmic flow of soft chattering whistles; the vigour of the performance is marked by an erect posture, with throat hackles bristling and drooping, quivering wings. The mimicry is expert; but, as seems to

be the case in most mimicry, the calls are imitated as they are heard - that is to say the imitation of a call sounds like the call in the distance rather than the sound of a bird calling where the Starling is perched. Wader and Gull calls are popular with our local birds: the example of song given includes mimicry of Grey Partridge, Swallow, Common Gull, Lapwing and Curlew calls. Birds will also copy electronic noises, car alarms and human whistles; one of our local birds produces a copy of the shrieks of children playing in the schoolyard down the road. Song can be heard at any time of year, especially on sunny mornings, though it is only occcasional in June and July. Alarm calls include a variety of sharp whistles to scolding churrs and rattles.

## SPARROWS - PASSERIDAE

**House Sparrow**   *Passer domesticus*                                          1,2
A gregarious and vocal bird, the House Sparrow produces a variety of chirping and churring notes, often delivered in long passages of monotonously regular repetition or run together into faster chirruping trills when birds are excited. The male's song is a regularly repeated silvery chirping note (1,12). Birds call with a rattling churr when alarmed or taking flight.

**Tree Sparrow**   *Passer montanus*                                             1,43
Very similar to the House Sparrow in sound and vocal behaviour, the Tree Sparrow's calls tend to be sharper and some calls have a characteristic metallic tone. Males sing with a repeated silvery chirrup like the House Sparrow, but are more prone to introduce variations and sometimes half-warbled phrases. The flight call is a distinctive 'tek, tek'.

## FINCHES - FRINGILLIDAE

In general behaviour the finches fall into two groups and this is reflected to a large extent in vocal behaviour. The fringilline finches, the Chaffinch and the Brambling, while forming flocks in winter, spend the Spring and Summer in pairs with mutually exclusive feeding and breeding territories; males can be territorially aggressive and sing loud stereotyped songs. The cardueline finches, which covers the other species here, tend to be more sociable throughout the year and usually breed in loose colonies. Birds within a party or flock frequently call with such a variety of motifs that it sounds like singing. And the male's full song tends to be a more intense and slightly more formal elaboration of such calling; the songs of these finches tend to be quieter and do not carry as far as that of the Chaffinch. Many of the cardueline species are birds of more open habitats, or the woodland edge, and song flights are frequent.

**Chaffinch**   *Fringilla coelebs*                                    1,25;1,68
Male Chaffinches begin to take up territories and sing from the early Spring, around the end of February; from then until around June, birds sing frequently and often for extended periods, after which song becomes occasional. The song is typically a descending series of short trills, often accelerating in tempo, in distinct sections, with a terminal flourish, the whole lasting 2 to 3 seconds; birds deliver these songs at regular intervals, at a rate of between 5 and 9 per minute (1,25). Each song is formally precise and is usually repeated for a while, then the bird changes to a different song from his repertoire, possibly in response to a neighbouring male's singing. Full song is loud and carries well; a softer, continuous warbling subsong is often heard in early Spring (1,68) and half-hearted versions of the full song later in the Summer. The Chaffinch is well studied vocally and has quite a vocabulary of distinct calls. A typical finch contact call, a soft, full 'chu' or 'chiff', is often given perched and in flight (1,25); this is usually repeated several times, but unlike similar calls from some other finches, not with any formal rhythm. A sharp 'chink', often given as a double note is heard for most of the year; birds on territory frequently repeat this call at short intervals for lengthy periods, and the call becomes slightly more strident when a bird is alarmed. A rising 'wheet', again often given as a double note, sometimes with a hint of a trill in the voice, is frequent from perched birds. In some areas a short churring trill, repeated at intervals, is common from territorial males.

**Brambling**   *Fringilla montifringilla*
Though closely related to the Chaffinch, the Brambling has a very different form of song, more akin to the wheezing trill of a Greenfinch. Males repeat a rattling or wheezing trill of about 1 second, which may sound like 'tchrrree' or 'dzwee' with a nasal tone to it. The most characteristic calls are a rising 'tchway', a slightly Dunnock-like, short, whistled 'twee' and a terse, repeated 'chuk'.

**Serin**   *Serinus serinus*
A tinkling series of notes, not unlike a Goldfinch, but more light-weight and rapid is the mark of the Serin; this may occur in a short burst, often descending slightly in pitch, as a call or in more intense passages of song, with something of a rapid chittering sound, often given in songflight.

Serins also have a distinctive, short, nasal 'cherr' call, sometimes given as a double note motif, reminiscent of a Siskin.

**Greenfinch**   *Carduelis chloris*                                         1,21
Precisely enunciated trills and wheezes are characteristic of the Green-finch. Greenfinches call with a slightly wheezy 'too-ee', often heard in early Spring, a clear 'teu-teu-teu', a drawn-out wheezing 'dwee' and rolling, trilled sequences of notes like the 'chu' of the Chaffinch. Most of these calls are used by singing males; song is a more elaborate, almost continuous series of varied trills and some wheezes, but as in many of the other cardueline species song is not always distinct from calling. Song is usually given from a prominent perch, and in a fluttering song flight circling back to the same perch or another near by. Generally a vocal bird, particularly in Spring and Summer, Greenfinches tend to work in small parties, flocking in Winter, and breed in loose colonies.

**Goldfinch**   *Carduelis carduelis*                                        1,19
Like the Greenfinch, Goldfinches are generally vocal birds, usually foraging and travelling in small parties, joining up with mixed flocks in Winter and breeding in small groups. Birds call frequently with short bursts of fluent, liquid twittering or warbling, often sounding like 'whit-a-whit', which, when delivered more intensely and regularly, is indistin-guishable from song. Singing birds tend to deliver more elaborate and formal (though, on first hearing it sounds meandering) snatches of such twittering, often including Greenfinch-like trills, usually lasting 2 to 4 seconds, but sometimes in an extended burst of up to 10 seconds. Such birds, singing or calling from a perch, tend to sing vigorously for a minute or two, then suddenly take flight. Birds also call readily in flight with 'whit-a-whit' type calls and a call similar to the Chaffinch's 'chu', but shorter and thinner sounding, usually in short rhythmic runs. Birds are vocal throughout the year, but regular song is heard in Spring and Summer. There are various other distinct calls heard occasionally, in-cluding a zinging 'zwee', rising in pitch.

**Siskin**   *Carduelis spinus*                                              1,86
Siskins are generally vocal birds and often call with many variations on a descending, plaintive-sounding 'teu' and a rising, wheezy 'teuy' or 'turlee'; runs of Chaffinch-like 'chu's, but a little harder-sounding and in a slightly scratchier voice, are frequent as a bird takes flight and in flight. Flocks in Winter often call with chattering motifs in a scratchy voice. Singing males deliver runs of vigorous twittering or warbling, seemingly of a random structure but usually with formally arranged elements from

the repertoire of each individual and usually including trills, sweet wheezes and fluent mimicry. Each burst usually lasts 10 to 20 seconds, followed by a short interval in which the bird may give several 'teu' or 'turlee' calls, but sometimes lasting over a minute - the example given in the audio is particularly long. Song may be from a prominent perch, but as the Spring advances is frequent in a fluttering, often circular song flight. Song becomes less frequent from June.

**Linnet**   *Carduelis cannabina*                                    1,39;1,41
Linnets, like many of the other cardueline species are very social and vocal; Linnets in particular are prone to singing in snatches in almost any circumstances and again it is not always easy to draw a distinction between calls and song. Males sing in short bursts of a kind of warble, pleasantly melodious, with a very slight wheezing tone to the voice and short intervals between each song; the songs are not particularly loud or far-carrying (1,41). Song can be heard at virtually any time of year but is most frequent and intense in the Spring and is usually from a perch, but is sometimes given in flight. A wheezy 'teoo-wee' call frequently accompanies song and often crops up in a song; quite a hard 'chic', usually repeated, and often given in a rhythmic series like a rattling trill is used for contact, in flight and frequently by birds feeding in a flock (1,39). Also heard is a Dunnock-like 'cheep', which may be used in alarm.

**Twite**   *Carduelis flavirostris*                                        2,19
The Twite is a vocal bird like its close relative, the Linnet, and sounds something like the Linnet, but with a more nasal twang to its voice and a less melodious song. Characteristic calls include a short 'tchweet' and a more drawn-out 'tchway' or frequently something like 'tchway-de-wee'; song is usually a series of phrases built around these or similar calls, with short intervals between - not so elaborate as a Linnet's song. Song is heard in Spring and Summer. In contact and flight, a similar 'chic' to the Linnet, but with quite a distinct softer tone, is used and is usually repeated in similar runs to the Linnet.

**Redpoll**   *Carduelis flammea*                                          1,92
Redpolls are a sociable species usually encountered in flocks and breeding in loose colonies; they tend to be quite vocal much of the time, particularly so in Spring and Summer. Particularly distinctive is a purring trill flight-call repeated as the main element in the bird's song flight; this is often accompanied by various 'chi-chi-chi' notes often run together as a trill. Displaying birds are very vocal, but restless, frequently

taking to the wing in a bouncing display flight. Birds singing from a perch elaborate on a variety of 'chi-chi-chi' and 'teu-teu-teu' calls, often forming trills; there is often a slightly scratchy wheeziness to the bird's tone of voice. Birds also call with a clear 'tuee', less plaintive than the similar call of the Siskin.

**Common Crossbill**   *Loxia curvirostra*                                  1,88
Crossbills are very gregarious birds, often forming large flocks in Winter, but still remaining in feeding groups of around 2 to 10 birds. The most frequent call, a kind of 'jip' of variable tone and volume is given in contact, as a flight call and often as an element in the song; a rich 'teu' is heard frequently and seems to have territorial (though Crossbills are not strictly territorial birds), or possibly aggressive, significance. In Spring and Summer a frequently-repeated call sounding like 'situ, sit-situ' is heard from young birds in feeding parties. Full song is not easy to recognise in this species and a soft twittering or warbling subsong, usually interspersed with louder whistles, is frequently heard in the second half of the year. Crossbills breed early in the year, sometimes from January or February, and as the flocking birds begin to form pairs in the late Autumn, song becomes more intense and formal but not particularly loud, consisting in bursts of notes, often repeated, with a hint of the Linnet's melodiousness, with short intervals between the bursts. The notes and song-phrases show a wide variety and song flights become frequent as courtship intensifies; the male's full song is characteristically a slightly longer, louder and more complex development and is heard occasionally in the late Winter and early Spring.

**Scottish Crossbill**   *Loxia scotica*
Closely related to the Common Crossbill (and only recently regarded as a separate species) the Scottish Crossbill's vocalisation differs very little. It has been said that the 'jip' call has become a loud, distinctive 'jup' in the Scottish population.

**Bullfinch**   *Pyrrhula pyrrhula*                                  1,64;1,65
Bullfinches are less gregarious and vociferous than the other cardueline species. Their usual call is a short, whistled 'peu' (1,65); this is often given very softly in contact and is easily overlooked, but can be quite forceful, probably when a bird is alarmed. Males have a soft song (it can be heard in the background towards the end of 1,64) and is usually a short series of slightly creaky, piped notes, descending in pitch and repeated at intervals. They also occasionally deliver a very

99

soft subsong (1,65) which can be a more elaborate and continuous warbling. Song may be heard from the late Winter through to early Summer.

**Hawfinch**   *Coccothraustes coccothraustes*                              1,71
Hawfinches are very secretive and wary birds, whose vocalisation is not well known. Most characteristic and frequently-heard is an explosive 'tzik' call, which may be used for contact, but also probably in alarm. Birds also call with a high, thin 'tee's and 'zee's. Song is rarely heard, but it seems that birds sing repeated, rather simple twittering notes, often variations of the calls, from a high perch, but not with any power; a very soft slightly gutteral warbling has also been heard. Song is most frequent in February and March. Courtship display in this species involves elaborate ritualised movements and posturing.

# BUNTINGS - EMBERIZIDAE

Buntings, generally birds of open habitats, are fairly vocal and tend to call frequently and repeat stereotyped songs for fairly long periods in the breeding season.

**Lapland Bunting**   *Calcarius lapponicus*
Lapland Buntings call with a soft, terse 'teu', not as deep as the Bullfinch but similar, often accompanied by some sweet, slightly wheezy notes; the contact and flight note is like the finches a repeated brief 'tchi', rather like the Redpoll, but not so rapidly repeated or trilled and a slightly trilled 'ticky-tic-tic' is frequently heard. The male's song is a short warble of slightly wheezy and scratchy notes, often including some purer, whistled notes suggestive of the Linnet's song.

**Snow Bunting**   *Plectrophenax nivalis*
The calls of the Snow Bunting include a plaintive 'teu', resembling the similar call of the Siskin more than the Lapland Bunting, but not so drawn-out, and a short, rattling trill, reminiscent of the Redpoll or the Lesser Whitethroat; these may be accompanied by a wheezy 'sichew' or similar motif. The male's song, often given in song flight, is a short, quite hurried warble and varies between individuals, sometimes reminiscent of a Whitethroat and sometimes more melodious, suggesting a Skylark.

**Yellowhammer**   *Emberiza citrinella*                              1,34
The languid song of the Yellowhammer, repeated at intervals for long periods with its insect-like building repetition of notes is redolent of

Summer for me. Birds usually have several different song types and repeat one song for a while before changing to another; all songs tend to consist of a rhythmic series of repeated notes ending in a drawn-out, high-pitched wheeze, though often the ending is left out. The traditional mnemonic for the song's rhythm is 'a little bit of bread and no chee-eese'. Song can be heard at any time of the day from the early Spring through to high Summer. Calls include a short 'chu', a very abrupt 'zit', a slightly more drawn out 'zee' and a soft rippling 'trrlp', most frequently heard in Winter and forming the basis of snatches of subsong heard from Winter flocks.

**Cirl Bunting**  *Emberiza cirlus*
The song of the Cirl Bunting is formally very similar to the Yellow-hammer's, but lacks the drawn-out ending, has a slightly more metallic timbre and shows greater variety in the notes used for different song types; in some songs the notes are repeated more rapidly, beginning to sound like the trill of the Lesser Whitethroat. Each song lasts around 2 to 3 seconds and they are delivered at a rate of about 4 or 5 to the minute; song can be heard from the early Spring right through to the Autumn. Calls include a very thin, high-pitched, descending 'tseu', a fuller, shorter 'teu' and a repeated 'tchi-tchi', reminiscent of the Redpoll.

**Reed Bunting**  *Emberiza schoeniclus*　　　　　　　　　2,28;2,32;2,34
Male Reed Buntings have formally very simple territorial songs, usually consisting of a run of 3 or 4 short notes, often with intervals of no more than a few seconds between subsequent deliveries; also one or more of the notes is usually trilled (2,28;2,34). Males sing from fairly low perches, such as the top of a low bush, and can be heard from early Spring through to early Summer. The usual call is a descending 'tsew', sometimes with a disyllabic emphasis, sounding more like 'tsee-you' (2,32).

**Corn Bunting**  *Miliaria calandra*　　　　　　　　　　　　　　1,35
In areas where Corn Buntings breed, the song of the male is heard persistently through the day from early Spring to mid Summer, and occasionally during the Autumn and Winter. Males are polygamous and sing from prominent perches, usually a fence-post, low bush or telephone-pole in their open habitat, where they can keep an eye on their territories. The song is a stereotyped, accelerating series of jangling notes, beginning with some hesitant clicks, and often compared to the sound of a bunch of keys being shaken. Each song lasts about 2 seconds

and around 6 to 8 songs are delivered per minute. Although the song appears to have no structure to our ears, when a recording is played back at half speed, a series of more or less distinct phrases becomes apparent. Calls include an abrupt 'tchk', rather like the opening notes of the song, and various short grating or churring notes, often given in alarm.

Checklist

This list only covers the species described in this book. For a comprehensive checklist, see *Collins Field Guide to the Birds of Britain & Europe* by Roger Tory Peterson, Guy Mountfort and P.A.D. Hollom.

- ... Red-throated Diver   *Gavia stellata*
- ... Black-throated Diver   *Gavia arctica*
- ... Great Northern Diver   *Gavia immer*
- ... Little Grebe   *Tachybaptus ruficollis*
- ... Great Crested Grebe   *Podiceps cristatus*
- ... Red-necked Grebe   *Podiceps grisegena*
- ... Slavonian Grebe   *Podiceps auritus*
- ... Black-necked Grebe   *Podiceps nigricollis*
- ... Fulmar   *Fulmarus glacialis*
- ... Manx Shearwater   *Puffinus puffinus*
- ... Storm Petrel   *Hydrobates pelagicus*
- ... Leach's Petrel   *Oceanodroma leucorhoa*
- ... Gannet   *Sula bassana*
- ... Cormorant   *Phalacrocorax carbo*
- ... Shag   *Phalacrocorax aristotelis*
- ... Bittern   *Botaurus stellaris*
- ... Grey Heron   *Ardea cinerea*
- ... Mute Swan   *Cygnus olor*
- ... Bewick's Swan   *Cygnus columbianus*
- ... Whooper Swan   *Cygnus cygnus*
- ... Bean Goose   *Anser fabalis*
- ... Pink-footed Goose   *Anser brachyrhynchus*
- ... White-fronted Goose   *Anser albifrons*
- ... Greylag Goose   *Anser anser*
- ... Canada Goose   *Branta canadensis*
- ... Barnacle Goose   *Branta leucopsis*
- ... Brent Goose   *Branta bernicla*
- ... Shelduck   *Tadorna tadorna*
- ... Mandarin   *Aix galericulata*
- ... Wigeon   *Anas penelope*
- ... Gadwall   *Anas strepera*
- ... Teal   *Anas crecca*
- ... Mallard   *Anas platyrhynchos*
- ... Pintail   *Anas acuta*

... Garganey *Anas querquedula*
... Shoveler *Anas clypeata*
... Pochard *Aythya ferina*
... Tufted Duck *Aythya fuligula*
... Scaup *Aythya marila*
... Eider *Somateria mollissima*
... Long-tailed Duck *Clangula hyemalis*
... Common Scoter *Melanitta nigra*
... Velvet Scoter *Melanitta fusca*
... Goldeneye *Bucephala clangula*
... Red-breasted Merganser *Mergus serrator*
... Goosander *Mergus merganser*
... Honey Buzzard *Pernis apivorus*
... Red Kite *Milvus milvus*
... White-tailed Eagle *Haliaeetus albicilla*
... Marsh Harrier *Circus aeruginosus*
... Hen Harrier *Circus cyaneus*
... Montagu's Harrier *Circus pygargus*
... Goshawk *Accipiter gentilis*
... Sparrowhawk *Accipiter nisus*
... Buzzard *Buteo buteo*
... Rough-legged Buzzard *Buteo lagopus*
... Golden Eagle *Aquila chrysaetos*
... Osprey *Pandion haliaetus*
... Kestrel *Falco tinnunculus*
... Merlin *Falco columbarius*
... Hobby *Falco subbuteo*
... Gyrfalcon *Falco rusticolus*
... Peregrine Falcon *Falco peregrinus*
... Red (or Willow) Grouse *Lagopus lagopus*
... Ptarmigan *Lagopus mutus*
... Black Grouse *Tetrao tetrix*
... Capercaillie *Tetrao urogallus*
... Red-legged Partridge *Alectoris rufa*
... Grey Partridge *Perdix perdix*
... Quail *Coturnix coturnix*
... Pheasant *Phasianus colchicus*
... Golden Pheasant *Chrysolophus pictus*
... Water Rail *Rallus aquaticus*
... Spotted Crake *Porzana porzana*

... Corncrake    *Crex crex*
... Moorhen    *Gallinula chloropus*
... Coot    *Fulica atra*
... Oystercatcher    *Haematopus ostralegus*
... Avocet    *Recurvirostra avosetta*
... Stone-curlew    *Burhinus oedicnemus*
... Little Ringed Plover    *Charadrius dubius*
... Ringed Plover    *Charadrius hiaticula*
... Kentish Plover    *Charadrius alexandrinus*
... Dotterel    *Charadrius morinellus*
... Golden Plover    *Pluvialis apricaria*
... Grey Plover    *Pluvialis squatarola*
... Lapwing    *Vanellus vanellus*
... Knot    *Calidris canutus*
... Sanderling    *Calidris alba*
... Little Stint    *Calidris minuta*
... Temminck's Stint    *Calidris temminckii*
... Purple Sandpiper    *Calidris maritima*
... Dunlin    *Calidris alpina*
... Ruff    *Philomachus pugnax*
... Jack Snipe    *Lymnocryptes minimus*
... Snipe    *Gallinago gallinago*
... Woodcock    *Scolopax rusticola*
... Black-tailed Godwit    *Limosa limosa*
... Bar-tailed Godwit    *Limosa lapponica*
... Whimbrel    *Numenius phaeopus*
... Curlew    *Numenius arquata*
... Spotted Redshank    *Tringa erythropus*
... Redshank    *Tringa totanus*
... Greenshank    *Tringa nebularia*
... Green Sandpiper    *Tringa ochropus*
... Wood Sandpiper    *Tringa glareola*
... Common Sandpiper    *Actitis hypoleucos*
... Turnstone    *Arenaria interpres*
... Red-necked Phalarope    *Phalaropus lobatus*
... Arctic Skua    *Stercorarius parasiticus*
... Long-tailed Skua    *Stercorarius longicaudus*
... Great Skua    *Stercorarius skua*
... Mediteranean Gull    *Larus melanocephalus*
... Little Gull    *Larus minutus*

... Black-headed Gull   *Larus ridibundus*
... Common Gull   *Larus canus*
... Lesser Black-backed Gull   *Larus fuscus*
... Herring Gull   *Larus argentatus*
... Great Black-backed Gull   *Larus marinus*
... Kittiwake   *Rissa tridactyla*
... Sandwich Tern   *Sterna sandvicensis*
... Roseate Tern   *Sterna dougallii*
... Common Tern   *Sterna hirundo*
... Arctic Tern   *Sterna paradisaea*
... Little Tern   *Sterna albifrons*
... Black Tern   *Chlidonias niger*
... Guillemot   *Uria aalge*
... Razorbill   *Alca torda*
... Black Guillemot   *Cepphus grylle*
... Little Auk   *Alle alle*
... Puffin   *Fratercula arctica*
... Rock Dove/Feral Pigeon   *Columba livia*
... Stock Dove   *Columba oenas*
... Woodpigeon   *Columba palumbus*
... Collared Dove   *Streptopelia decaocto*
... Turtle Dove   *Streptopelia turtur*
... Ring-necked Parakeet   *Psittacula krameri*
... Cuckoo   *Cuculus canorus*
... Barn Owl   *Tyto alba*
... Snowy Owl   *Nyctea scandiaca*
... Little Owl   *Athene noctua*
... Tawny Owl   *Strix aluco*
... Long-eared Owl   *Asio otus*
... Short-eared Owl   *Asio flammeus*
... Nightjar   *Caprimulgus europaeus*
... Swift   *Apus apus*
... Kingfisher   *Alcedo atthis*
... Hoopoe   *Upupa epops*
... Wryneck   *Jynx torquilla*
... Green Woodpecker   *Picus viridis*
... Great Spotted Woodpecker   *Dendrocopos major*
... Lesser Spotted Woodpecker   *Dendrocopos minor*
... Woodlark   *Lullula arborea*
... Skylark   *Alauda arvensis*

... Shore Lark   *Eremophila alpestris*
... Sand Martin   *Riparia riparia*
... Swallow   *Hirundo rustica*
... House Martin   *Delichon urbica*
... Tree Pipit   *Anthus trivialis*
... Meadow Pipit   *Anthus pratensis*
... Rock Pipit   *Anthus petrosus*
... Yellow Wagtail   *Motacilla flava*
... Grey Wagtail   *Motacilla cinerea*
... Pied Wagtail   *Motacilla alba*
... Waxwing   *Bombycilla garrulus*
... Dipper   *Cinclus cinclus*
... Wren   *Troglodytes troglodytes*
... Dunnock   *Prunella modularis*
... Robin   *Erithacus rubecula*
... Nightingale   *Luscinia megarhynchos*
... Bluethroat   *Luscinia svecica*
... Black Redstart   *Phoenicurus ochruros*
... Redstart   *Phoenicurus phoenicurus*
... Winchat   *Saxicola rubetra*
... Stonechat   *Saxicola torquata*
... Wheatear   *Oenanthe oenanthe*
... Ring Ouzel   *Turdus torquatus*
... Blackbird   *Turdus merula*
... Fieldfare   *Turdus pilaris*
... Song Thrush   *Turdus philomelos*
... Redwing   *Turdus iliacus*
... Mistle Thrush   *Turdus viscivorus*
... Cetti's Warbler   *Cettia cetti*
... Grasshopper Warbler   *Locustella naevia*
... Savi's Warbler   *Locustella luscinioides*
... Sedge Warbler   *Acrocephalus schoenobaenus*
... Marsh Warbler   *Acrocephalus palustris*
... Reed Warbler   *Acrocephalus scirpaceus*
... Dartford Warbler   *Sylvia undata*
... Lesser Whitethroat   *Sylvia curruca*
... Whitethroat   *Sylvia communis*
... Garden Warbler   *Sylvia borin*
... Blackcap   *Sylvia atricapilla*
... Wood Warbler   *Phylloscopus sibilatrix*

... Chiffchaff *Phylloscopus collybita*
... Willow Warbler *Phylloscopus trochilus*
... Goldcrest *Regulus regulus*
... Firecrest *Regulus ignicapillus*
... Spotted Flycatcher *Muscicapa striata*
... Pied Flycatcher *Ficedula hypoleuca*
... Bearded Tit *Panurus biarmicus*
... Long-tailed Tit *Aegithalos caudatus*
... Marsh Tit *Parus palustris*
... Willow Tit *Parus montanus*
... Crested Tit *Parus cristatus*
... Coal Tit *Parus ater*
... Blue Tit *Parus caeruleus*
... Great Tit *Parus major*
... Nuthatch *Sitta europaea*
... Treecreeper *Certhia familiaris*
... Golden Oriole *Oriolus oriolus*
... Red-backed Shrike *Lanius collurio*
... Great Grey Shrike *Lanius excubitor*
... Jay *Garrulus glandarius*
... Magpie *Pica pica*
... Chough *Pyrrhocorax pyrrhocorax*
... Jackdaw *Corvus monedula*
... Rook *Corvus frugilegus*
... Carrion/Hooded Crow *Corvus corone*
... Raven *Corvus corax*
... Starling *Sturnus vulgaris*
... House Sparrow *Passer domesticus*
... Tree Sparrow *Passer montanus*
... Chaffinch *Fringilla coelebs*
... Brambling *Fringilla montifringilla*
... Serin *Serinus serinus*
... Greenfinch *Carduelis chloris*
... Goldfinch *Carduelis carduelis*
... Siskin *Carduelis spinus*
... Linnet *Carduelis cannabina*
... Twite *Carduelis flavirostris*
... Redpoll *Carduelis flammea*
... Common Crossbill *Loxia curvirostra*
... Scottish Crossbill *Loxia scotica*

... Bullfinch *Pyrrhula pyrrhula*
... Hawfinch *Coccothraustes coccothraustes*
... Lapland Bunting *Calcarius lapponicus*
... Snow Bunting *Plectrophenax nivalis*
... Yellowhammer *Emberiza citrinella*
... Cirl Bunting *Emberiza cirlus*
... Reed Bunting *Emberiza schoeniclus*
... Corn Bunting *Miliaria calandra*

# Index

The numbers in this index relate to the page number in the book, followed by the disc and track number on the CD

NOTES

NOTES

NOTES

NOTES

NOTES